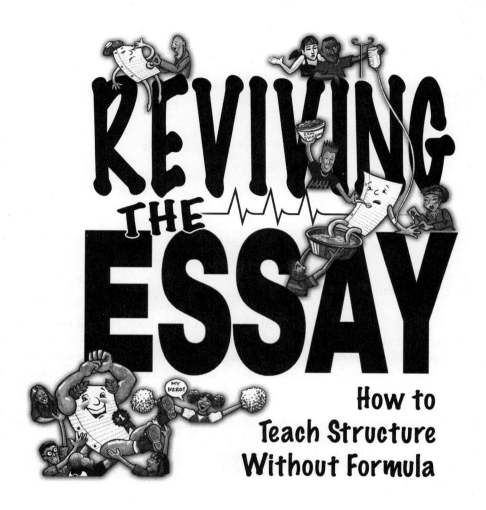

REVIVING THE ESSAY

How to Teach Structure Without Formula

BY GRETCHEN BERNABEI

DISCOVER WRITING PRESS

Discover Writing Press
P.O. Box 264
Shoreham, Vermont 05770
1-800-613-8055
www.discoverwriting.com

Cover art by Robert Rehm
Book design by Bookwrights

ISBN# 1-931492-13-1

Library of Congress Control Number: 2004111631

05 06 07 08 09 10 9 8 7 6 5 4 3 2 1

For information on seminars and more lesson plans call 1-800-613-8055
or visit our website at www.discoverwriting.com

-For Matilde and Johnny

Table of Contents

Chapter 3. Experimenting with Thick Description

Chapter 4. Crafting The Essay for a Reader's Ears

Foreword

Every house probably has a stash of trick birthday candles—you know, the kind that seem to go out, sputter for a second, and then relight. It's usually best not to use all trick candles on a cake, only one or two, to confuse the birthday boy or girl, who gathers in a second lungful of air and tries again. Most people get it by the third try.

It occurs to me that the tight five paragraph school essay bears a resemblance to these trick candles. No matter how hard we try to extinguish it, no matter how many times critics like Janet Emig have pointed out its limitations, no matter how many times we refill our lungs—it still springs back to life.

The standards movement has given it new life. As George Hillocks has painfully demonstrated, state assessment programs seem to evoke the five-paragraph formula no matter what kind of writing is being tested. So we get phony-sounding compositions that begin like this:

With all the crime and injustice in the world today, many young people need a hero or heroine to look up to. They need someone they can depend on and who can show them the difference between right and wrong. There are many important people in the world today who are good examples for kids, but the person I count on when I am having a rough time is someone very close to me who is easy to reach when I need her. My grandma, with her unique qualities and virtues has influenced me the most in my life.

I recently heard of an educational consultant in Colorado who was pulling four figures/day for showing teachers how the hamburger composition works. There's the top bun (the opening paragraph), the meat (the middle three paragraphs), and the bottom bun (the closing paragraph). The way I look at it, this approach is not simply an insult to students; it's an insult to hamburgers, which, after all, come in a lot of varieties—double cheese, cheese and bacon, etc.

The book you now hold, Gretchen Bernabei's *Reviving the Essay*, does more than any other book I know, to help teachers reimagine what an essay can be. I suspect that it will have more impact than many earlier critiques because it really offers alternatives, dozens of inviting opportunities for students to develop their thinking. For me a true measure of a great teaching book (like Kirby and Liner's *Inside Out* or Heard's *Writing Toward Home*) is their capacity to motivate, that gut feeling that says "I'd like to try this." This book passes that test.

It might seem paradoxical that a book devoted to revising the essay should be composed of so many lessons. After all, didn't Montaigne himself celebrate the "frenzy" of his own writing process. Yes, but he had also internalized the models of his mentors: Plutarch, Plato, Seneca. Not to mention that he was, after all, a lawyer, skilled at the kind of discourse he was subverting. He may have claimed that he was simply following the natural flow of his mind, but that mind was fully stocked.

Gretchen Bernabei recognized that the proper response to the narrow—dare I say anal—school essay, is not to disregard form and structure. It is not to simply create an open space for the "natural" flow of thought. Instead it is to replace one pattern with dozens of patterns. As teachers, we do not create a sense of possibility by simply effacing ourselves, by offering "freedom" without any guidance for how that freedom could be used. This simply inverts the problem, replacing rigidity with passive openness.

Instead, she offers a series of guided invitations that engage students with various patterns of development. She helps develop a repertoire of possibilities that can be altered, combined, even subverted and parodied. Creativity comes not from a mind freed of patterns, but from one supercharged with patterns.

It is especially gratifying for me to write a foreword to this book, as an earlier monograph I wrote has some role in its creation. What serendipidy to think that my short book, with miniscule sales, long out of print, could have this effect. And then I thought of Montaigne himself, writing in his tower. Could he ever have imagined, in his wildest dreams, that his own essays would, four hundred years after their publication, be such favorites of my father who would read them aloud in the late afternoon as he paced the floor of our house. And could my father have imagined the circuit that would lead from his reading, via my monograph, to this book.

It makes me think that the essay itself, as Montaigne imagined it, is the real spark that can't be extinguished.

Thomas Newkirk
Durham, NH

Acknowledgments

I'm so grateful for the work of the following people.

My most prized mentors: Joyce Armstrong Carroll, Edward Wilson, Dan Kirby, Gabrielle Rico, and Peter Medway.

My favorite teachers I've never met: Thomas Newkirk, Harvey Daniels, Lev Vygotsky, Frank Smith, Katie Wood Ray, Jim Burke, Nancie Atwell, Clifford Geertz, and Harry Noden.

My colleagues who share the English workroom at O'Connor High School and who influence my thinking daily, especially Cyndi Pina, Kristy Truss, Marcus Goodyear, Barbara Edens, and Jann Fractor.

Colleagues from my town who have compared notes with me and continue to share their excitement and love of teaching kids: Jayne Hover, Rebecca Shapiro, Michele Brinkley, Carol Siskovic, Suzi Lockamy, Michael Guevara, Laura Coindreau, Gary Degerstrom, Georgia Edwards, Heather Farmer, Sharon Christensen, Susan Sabino, Anna Rendon, Jo Ann Tschirhart, Darla White, Barbara Mayers, Jodi Ramos, Katy Van Winkle, Caroline McCarthy, Liz Ozuna, Becky Hoag, Elaine Asbell, and Jenny Guerrero, and our Main Brain Mama, Patricia S. Gray.

Colleagues from around Texas who continue the work and who have contributed to these lessons: Cathy D'Entrement, Jennifer Mykytiuk, Alana Morris, P. Tim Martindell, Mary Stockton, Kaye Price Hawkins, Karen Whitman, Mellissa Zipp, Nancy Klemme, Lara Wiedenfeld, Deanna Beauchamp, Sheila Wise, Diane Fisher, Becky Singley, Carole Trimpey, Pam John, Kathy McCutchen, Nancy Kahn, Carol Bradshaw, Carrie Strmiska, Suzanne Burke, Jeanne Cours, Mary Ellen Frick.

Students who have contributed text structures and artwork: John Kevin Cronin IV, Michael Williams, and Kathryn Legendre.

Special thanks to Cindy Tyroff, whose leadership in English education continues a culture of innovation in Northside ISD; Carolyn Denny, who was willing to think through and develop many of the activities in this book with me; my principal, Larry Martin, whose patience and support are what every teacher craves.

The incomparable, unflappable, "we're all soldiers in the same war" Barry Lane, whose example leads so many of us to temper our teaching and our lives with kindness and humor, as much as with reason and rigor.

Finally, my unending gratitude to three of the most brilliant friends anyone could hope for: Jeff Anderson, Kim Grauer, and Dottie Hall.

Gretchen Bernabei

Introduction

It's funny. You can be musing over several unrelated thoughts for days, for weeks, or in my case, for years, almost as though your thoughts are footpaths leading off in different directions. Then in an instant, with all the fanfare of a quiet click, the paths all intersect, changing your world. That's what happened to me. Here's my story.

Unrelated Footpath Number One

My school district supervisor, Cindy Tyroff, assigned my first task as instructional support teacher last year, a one-year stint away from my high school English classroom. "Read through these," she told me, indicating three foot-and-a-half-high piles of sample student essays, literary analyses from the high schools in our district.

"What am I looking for?" I studied her face for a clue.

"Oh, just see what you notice." I looked at the piles. I knew they were a mix, some A papers, some B papers, some others.

"What should I notice?" I studied her face some more, but it didn't help.

"See what we're doing well, and where we need to go from here," she said, disappearing into her office.

I heaved the first pile onto the desk and began to read. About barbarism in *Lord of the Flies*, about prejudice in *To Kill a Mockingbird*, about plots and characters and tone and symbolism. I wanted coffee. I wanted to commit hari-kari. I wanted another assignment.

Over the next several days, I read through more essays, and I saw some of the best of what we ask from students as they write essays about literature: punchy leads; correctly drawn MLA citations; multiple examples to support single points; apt vocabulary usage; clean organizational structures. But as I read some of our most "successful" papers, I also made myself a little page of notes that I didn't dare share. My notes felt like heresy, listing students' introductory comments that made me flinch, or phrases indicating that students had jumped through the required syntactical hoops without one shred of experiential understanding or heartfelt conviction. And the easiest of these to spot were endings: a second-person switchoff of quick advice, shallow counsel warning, for example, against barbarism. "So never be barbaric." Here are some examples:

> "Nothing Gold Can Stay" is a complete reminder of this and we must remember to live life to its fullest. Enjoy and take pleasure!

> The only way to prevent these disasters is to have an open mind towards others. Don't be too cocky.

> The most important moral in this novel is to accept that there will be adversity in your life and you will have to try to overcome it, even though it might be sad and difficult to succeed in.

The main theme is respect others and don't discriminate against them for being who they are.

Now since you have uncovered just a little bit of the crazy world of Odysseus what happened, characteristics and flaws, and things that just might freak you out. GO READ IT! You will be pleased.

But what exactly had we asked students to do? To conclude their thoughts. And these students had, clearly, but their endings didn't work, at least not for me. In fact, they revealed too much about the superficial nature of the essays.

What makes endings backfire? I thought back to a class I'd had with Dan Kirby. He had shown me how summing it all up in a "so here's what I learned" kind of way is too pat, too preachy, too thoughtless, too easy, and those endings ring false. They can ruin an otherwise thoughtful paper. But that's just the endings.

In short, these essays were deadly dull reading, but the drudgery seemed like *my* problem, not the problem of the essay writers or their teachers. Why? I quietly envied the polish I saw and thought, *These students' teachers know how to get finished-looking essays out of kids.* And the students had clearly accomplished their mission, completed the task, checked off every item on their essay to-do lists. I had worked in schools before where questioning these kinds of perfect-looking essays was only rewarded with cold, mute stares from the other teachers. So naturally, I felt a little funny about voicing my honest reaction: "These just don't seem very good."

An errand led me to my home high school, where I visited with colleagues before I returned to my essay-laden desk. As he was stepping into the lunchroom, Marcus Goodyear, a brilliant young AP teacher and friend, confided that he had spent the weekend dreading grading student essays. Finally, his wife Amy had said, "Marcus! You love reading. You love writing. You love those students. What do you hate so much about grading their essays?" Marcus looked at me and almost whispered, "They're boring."

Unrelated Footpath Number Two

Back in 1995, I spent six weeks at the Breadloaf School of English, studying the work of Lev Vygotsky. One among many of the lingering thoughts I took home had to do with the role of art. I had grown up on Aristotle and lofty thoughts about art (including literature) having to do with purifying my spirit through catharsis, but Vygotsky said something entirely different: We have art so that we can walk around it, staring, and seeing an expanded version of ourselves, of our human capacities, so that we can imagine ourselves in unimaginable situations. We have art so that we can rehearse, in a way, a future of the inexpressible.

There is the world, and there is us. Art shows us the world, and what we see changes us, giving us impetus to make changes in the world. It's a never-ending ricochet, helping us see how we fit into the world, extending who we are, helping us become people who can direct our wills, make plans, take action.

We have art for the same reasons we are compelled to slow down and look at car wrecks on the freeway. Oh sure, we don't want to be "rubber-neckers," but if you ever drive past a really bad car accident and don't stare, it's only because your self-discipline has overcome your natural compulsion to look. But why? What compels us to look? Maybe we think, *Because that could have been me.* Or *that could have been someone I love.* We have to know what it would look like, *if.*

Art is the same way. And this thought really changed for me the way I look at teaching literature. It taught me that barbarism in *Lord of the Flies* is more than the literary term *theme*; it's the *centerpiece* for coping with the school bus bullies of yesterday and for planning our votes for the world leaders of tomorrow. We teach literature because we have to survive.

Unrelated Footpath Number Three

As I was driving home from work, the familiar voice on National Public Radio mentioned something called "driveway moments." I listened:

> Maybe it's happened to you as it has to countless others . . .
> You're driving home, listening to a story on NPR. Suddenly, you find yourself in your driveway (or parking space or parking garage). Rather than turn the radio off, you stay in your car to hear the piece to the end.
> It's a Driveway Moment.

I almost laughed out loud. Yes! Many times I'd sat in my driveway, hoping my neighbors weren't noticing, listening to the words until the very last drop. Wouldn't our schools be different if the essays our students wrote had the same "Driveway Moment" effect?

The Footpaths Intersect

Cindy stopped by my desk, glancing at the essay piles. "How's it going?"

My confessions began. "I wasn't confused when I started, but now I am wondering about literary analyses. What are they supposed to be? Why do we have students write them? What do personal memories have to do with persuasive writing?"

We talked for a while, trying to arrive at the differences between real exploration and the school writing before us. "Tell them what you're going to tell, then tell it, then tell what you told."

I remembered a moment one evening, when I was driving to downtown San Antonio, the beer billboards glowing near the Alamodome. From the backseat piped up one ten-year-old voice, the successful result of the thorough, costly, nationally saturated, school antidrug DARE program:

Matilde: Mom, why do we have those there? Beer is a drug. Drugs are wrong.

Me: You're right.

Matilde: Then why do they let those signs go there? People will think it's okay to drink.

Me: I know. I wish our city would know what you kids know, and agree.

Matilde: How could they not?

Indeed. How could they not? Is the antidrug campaign just for school? I didn't want to purse my lips and say, "It doesn't work that way in the real world, honey." Why doesn't it? Why don't conversations and beliefs shape what we see on our highways? I think the bigger truth is that they do, and they will, but they won't if we don't have those conversations. Isn't that the nature of democracy?

What if we guided students who are writing school essays to think about what their moral is, how it connects to their life? Then, a possible new extension for the essay checklist might be to figure out what rules or laws we have about that particular issue. And to find out how our nation or community is addressing the same need the student is writing about. What dialogue are people having about that issue right now? Is the nation's work counter-productive to what the student thinks is needed? What if the student formed a real position about what should change?

School shouldn't stay within the walls of school. If we're asking students to connect to literature, why not use all the power of literature to make an impact on the world, not just comment on the state of the world? Not just to notice as observers, but to act on the world, to be participants, change-agents. I can't help but feel that whether it's a letter addressed to an elected official, or just the thoughtful ponderings of the student, all the essays students write could have an echo in the future, could be *conversation*.

Wouldn't it be a wonderful world if students were never asked to write bogus essays? And if they're writing meaningful pieces only, wouldn't those pieces routinely interact with the world?

Cindy disappeared into her office and reappeared, handing me a small, dark green book that looked erudite and boring. It was an ERIC monograph, published by the National Council of Teachers of English. "This might be interesting," she said.

I wasn't hopeful, but at least it gave me an excuse not to look at essays for a while. I was so wrong. Not about the erudite part, but about the boring part. It may have been the least boring piece of professional reading I'd done since my last encounter with Tom Romano. It was all about why school essays are boring, and about what real essays are sup-posed to be. I fell completely in love with the author of the book, Thomas Newkirk, and looked at the copyright date—1989. This had been in print since 1989, and we'd never stud-ied it? Why? Well, in Texas, what were we doing in 1989? We were just beginning the thir-teen-year run of the Texas Assessment of Academic Skills (TAAS) test, replete with rubrics that awarded high scores for formulaic writing and that had ended this year, 2002. I felt like Rip Van Winkle, ready to pick up where we left off, thirteen years ago.

My Mental Conversation with Thomas Newkirk

In his monograph, Thomas Newkirk told us about his daughter's school essay assignment and how she dreaded writing it. He looked at the assignment, and I'm sure it looked very similar to the assignments our students had faced, the ones that had produced the piles of essays before me. Newkirk wrote:

> We knew this writing was false, skilled at a superficial level, but false. It was not rooted in conviction, in the experience of the writer, and would therefore not enter the experience of the reader. It was what Jerome Harste has called a "textoid," an artificial creation. It was not an essay. The essay, I wanted to tell my daughter, was something different, something better, something looser, more personal, more playful.

Newkirk traced for me the genesis of that formulaic, front-end-loaded, schoolified essay. There it was, in Warriner's, just as I had learned it as a junior high school student. No wonder. I can read all the exciting, moving, meaningful pieces that American writers have been producing; I can sit in my driveway listening to language and thought from NPR; I can be mesmerized by articles in many commercial magazines; but when I start to assign students an essay, Warriner's training has stepped into the school spotlight. I fall back into teaching exactly the way I was taught, and a five-paragraph school essay assignment emerges.

So how do I ask students to write something different? How?

Newkirk showed me how the genre of "essay" began, as a form developed by Michel de Montaigne. I stopped at Barnes and Noble on the way home. Right there, on the first page of his *Essays*, Montaigne explained in 1580:

> My sole purpose in writing it has been a private and domestic one . . . I have intended it solely for the pleasure of my relatives and friends so that, when they have lost me—which they soon must—they may recover some features of my character and disposition, and thus keep the memory they have of me more completely and vividly alive.

"For the pleasure of my relatives and friends"? What student would feel that way about any of the essays before me? Would they want to leave those essays behind so that their loved ones would know them better? Most students I have taught would snort at the notion. So how do we convert the thinking students do about the literature they read into something personal and insightful about themselves?

The voice of Victoria Young echoed in my head. The director of our state's writing assessment, she had explained: "We're looking for a highly personal response which shows a genuine reaction to the prompt."

Was it possible? The state didn't want Warriner's any longer. They wanted Montaigne. What if we do what Thomas Newkirk urges, and reclaim the essay form? What if we threw the schoolified Warriner's essay out the window? What if our students wrote essays that could give one chills?

I had just been reading *If You Don't Feed the Teachers, They Eat the Students* by Neila A. Connors, and this connected: "One person with a true belief is worth more than ninety-nine with an interest." Surely a Montaignesque essay would reveal the heart and soul of the writer more than a Warrineresque one would. So how?

We have to take what we know and rebuild. Newkirk gave me the mental image for my shifting essay metaphor. The schoolified essay is a building, already finished at the beginning; the real essay is a journey that goes somewhere. Whereas the schoolified essay asks students to start with a conclusion, a thesis, and use the rest of the paper to "back it up," the real essay offers a journey for the reader, or it doesn't work: "As readers, we experience structure as movement through the text; we are propelled from paragraph to paragraph or we come to a standstill, moving on only out of a sense of duty" (14).

Who, not counting English teachers, has that strong a sense of duty? Not the listeners on NPR. Not the readers of any essays in the real world. And that standstill is precisely why those schoolified essays are horrible to read.

"We experience structure as movement through the text." Movement through the text. How do we show students how to move through a text? For students who begin writing at a standstill, we have to begin with something. What if we could map out where the movement goes?

So do we find a better formula? A whole lot of formulas, so students can choose? The animated discussion around the lunch table at O'Connor High School led my friend Marcus Goodyear to jot down this thought on a napkin:

> Teachers and writers often seem to be on a quest to find the ultimate template or genre or list of rules, devices, how-to, so that we can find the tools to explain our process, and train new artists. But artists don't start with a universal template or genre. Sometimes they/we start by imitating— using one work as a template. Every work of art must be so unique that it becomes its own template.

Thick Description

When Newkirk mentioned Clifford Geertz, something in my memory stirred. Thick description. The phrase had appeared in a call for manuscripts in *The English Journal* back in 1991, asking for classroom case studies. I rummaged through my files and found it. Here's what I saw:

> The heart of the "case" consists of what ethnographers call "thick description"; i.e., anecdotes, transcripts or reconstructed dialogue, writing samples, contextual details, field notes, and the like.

I remembered the whole 1991 experience. As a participant in the New Jersey Writing Project in Texas, led by Joyce Armstrong Carroll and Eddie Wilson, I had read that call for manuscripts and hauled it over to Eddie. "How much thick description would be enough?"

"How much do you want to include?"

"Do you think there'd be such a thing as too much?"

"I don't know . . . why don't you try it and see what happens?"

So I had constructed and submitted an article that was almost entirely thick description, alternating excerpts from a student journal with dialogue from my classroom. I remember experiencing writer's euphoria as the article practically wrote itself. I didn't need to say much, because the raw material did the talking. The article was published. I remember the writer's euphoria of seeing it in print.

Now I looked at Thomas Newkirk again. Had I used what I learned about thick description with my students? No, I had not. Not once in twelve years had it occurred to me to enliven student writing for readers' eyes by using what the National Council of Teachers of English considered a valuable readability tool. I couldn't slap my forehead hard enough.

In fact, it might be time to rethink art, literature, and essay writing, and to use everything we know as we reshape what it is we're asking students to do.

Vygotsky points out that art has a functional role in our world. The world moves us; we, in turn, move it. We are acted on by our environment; we act on it. It shapes us; we shape it. Something we read moves us; we move to influence someone else. This creates the constant push-pull of meaning and our lives. We're not just *finding* meaning in our lives. We're *shaping our world* because of the meanings that we find. Literature and all art are powerful tools for change.

As teachers, we are charged with the responsibility of leading students to make meaning in whatever is before them, whether it is literature, world events, or gossip, and to act on that meaning. To change the world. Yet our habit of teaching rigid, passive, formula essays or lessons only for school (not for the real world, honey) teaches students exactly how not to change a thing—how not to engage, how not to act on their world, how not to, for example, vote.

Some state assessments reward dead writing, schoolified writing, and so the writing programs in the schools of those states are guided by this. In Texas and a few other states, those years are finally gone.

So it looks to me like our work is clear. All the footpaths converged in my mind, synthesizing into these parts: There are four steps to writing a "driveway moment" kind of essay, not one of which is part of a schoolified essay:

1. Find your message, something that you believe.

2. Find (or invent) your structure.

3 Experiment with thick description, and design the presentation.

4. Try it on readers, and revise from there.

How? Those are the lessons that follow. Mr. Newkirk, you're on.

How Do I Use This Book?

Kids need three things in order to produce their most prized work: possibilities, freedom, and feedback. In our classrooms, if we assign the essay, and we choose the prompt, and we choose the structure, and we choose the feedback, we shouldn't really complain too much if we can't find the student anywhere in the essay. And we really have no right to complain if the essays all sound the same. Students have followed our directions.

Teachers need the same three things in order to produce our own most prized teaching: possibilities, freedom, and feedback. This book provides possibilities for teaching strategies all along the essay-writing path: step-by-step ways to show students how to address writing prompts; concrete ways to replace formula with possibilities of structure; models of ways to design a look and sound for the writing and reinvent prose; strategies for ways to listen to an essay and write for a reader's ear and to revise according to the feedback the writer sees.

The possibilities laid out in these lessons are accompanied by freedom. Every lesson has a brief introduction, followed by a "Teaching It" section, a transcription of one way that this lesson has been taught with students. Student samples from grades four through twelve are scattered throughout, with some teacher-written samples as well. The samples can serve as models, or as starting points, or as points of reference for teachers to see what other people's kids produced through these lessons. Teachers might choose combinations of lessons to try, and adapt them at will.

Finally, the most significant feedback we should heed comes from our own students. The lessons that work are the ones that produce writing that is more interesting, more lively. If variations of these lessons work better, then that's the feedback we should listen to and share with our colleagues. I'd love to see samples of what your students produce. Send some!

The book is divided into four chapters:

Chapter 1: Finding Your Message

What do students do when they're given a prompt? How can students collect their thoughts and come up with one really great thesis statement? Chapter 1 deals with finding a message for the essay. If your students are in the early stages of their essay writing, these lessons can help with the depth, focus, and believability of what their essay is going to say.

Chapter 2: Finding (or Inventing) Your Structure

Have the students settled on a message, and now wonder how to proceed? Chapter 2 will help with developing a plan for structuring their essay. Each lesson starts off with a graphic map of one organizational pattern. The lessons progress from the narrative structures that develop in the earliest writers to the more analytical and complex structures as abstract thought develops. Elementary students can use almost all of the structures successfully and shouldn't be confined to the first structures; likewise, the older students could make fine use of the structures all up and down the range of complexity.

Teachers are free to use the structures in any number of different ways, from freewriting to guided writing, as kernel essays or full essays. Models are given for both guided writing and kernel essays for each of the structures.

Each of these lessons is followed by a sample prompt, so that teachers might see what students would actually do with a prompt and that particular text structure. The prompts used in this chapter are taken from "Lightning in a Bottle," a CD compilation of prompts in English and Spanish, accompanied by photographs.

Chapter 3: Experimenting with Thick Description

Do the students have a message and a structure, and possibly a draft? Chapter 3 provides ways to dress up the essay with "thick description" by tinkering with chunks of text from the student's world, maybe weaving sound effects into it like an echo, or ribboning dialogue, poetry, or lyrics throughout, or framing it with a symbolic concrete object.

Chapter 4: Crafting The Essay for a Reader's Ears

The lessons in Chapter 4 can be used as revision strategies or prewriting visions about the role of the audience. This chapter focuses on getting an essay ready to be heard by others, on ways of getting the reader into the writer's skin.

In *Teaching the Universe of Discourse*, James Moffett said, "We educators are learning to do better and better some things that should not be done at all. We are rapidly perfecting error. Which is to say that I think we should heed better the feedback we get about the consequences of our own teaching actions."

Instead of doing better and better the things that should not be done at all, let's revive the essay—the real essay, NPR's essay, Newkirk's essay, Montaigne's essay. Let's offer models. Let's invite imitation. Let's celebrate invention. And let's get ready for the students to knock our socks off.

1

Finding Your Message

Sometimes students are given the freedom to dream up their own topic to develop into a more focused thesis, assertion, or opinion. But more often, teachers give students a prompt to write about. This prompt might be in the form of a quotation, a "thought for the day," a question, or a thesis statement. And sometimes the state delivers a prompt on a state writing assessment.

When students hunker down to "write to the prompt," often the prompt itself appears in their writing at least once, many times as both the beginning and ending of their essays, with only bland illustrations in between.

Think about it. A prompt like "Write about how people are affected by the choices they make" becomes an essay that begins, "People are affected by the choices they make." Sure, sometimes a slick lead can camouflage the bare-bones response, but the student may never stray from the prompt, sticking to it so much that the resulting essay is devoid of any surprises or discoveries. And even if the student writer does a convincing job of sounding genuine, the main thought of the essay came from somewhere outside the writer, from someone else.

Testing results confirm the need for the students to unify their essays with something internal. Victoria Young from the Texas Education Agency explained that an essay is more focused and coherent if its unifying theme is "one step away from the prompt." TEA staffer Muffet Livaudais explained further what "one step away from the prompt" means. From the prompt "Write about what makes you happy," a student had written about eating pizza, going to the mall, and playing baseball. The only relationship those parts had was to the prompt. Each of those things made the student happy, but the parts had no relationship to one another. This made the piece not coherent, and the writer would most likely only get a 1 or a 2 on a 4-point rubric. The student could have used these three ideas if they had been linked to some other unifying angle, like "doing things with my family makes me happy," and then gone on to focus on the family in each of those three activities.

So the first step in writing an essay has to be for the writer to chew on the prompt, to read and reread it, to digest it, to find the hard-won truth in it, or the paradox in it, or the human struggle within it. Teachers use the words "narrow the focus," but the meaning there doesn't translate to students. However, students do understand what it means to locate and identify one real belief, full of passion and experience, from the prompt.

The lessons in this chapter help students transform a prompt into something of their own, something true. The reader will notice and sit up.

Lesson 1:
Truisms

Students need guided practice in order to find a unifying message for their essays, a truth, a life lesson, a mystery about the world. They also need guidance to develop a feel for more compelling or interesting thoughts.

To practice finding these, photographs provide a useful training ground, especially with developing readers. Students may have difficulty reading printed text, but they read body language and situations much more easily. They can read a photograph and make insightful inferences about what they see.

This progression of exercises, developed by Jayne Hover and her fourth graders, leads students to find their own natural angle to a prompt. It begins with showing them prompts that accompany photographs and teaching them to read the parts of the photograph in order to see the connection. When students get pretty good at that step, they go on to create their own statements to accompany photographs, statements that "nail" a human truth in the photograph, a truism. The last step removes the photograph completely and challenges students to first read a typical prompt, and then to sketch a quick image. Then, looking at their own sketch, they write truisms.

Teaching It:

Step 1: Get familiar with truisms with photo

(Put a prompt with photograph on the overhead. See page 5 for an example. Cover the photograph.)
"Look at this sentence. Do you think it's true?"
(Uncover the photograph.)
"How does the picture relate?" (Let them comment.)
(Put another prompt with photograph on the overhead. Cover the photograph.)
"Read this statement. What picture could be there?"
(Do a couple like this.)

Step 2: Write truisms from photo

(Show photo with prompt covered.)
"What do you see going on in this photo?" (Let students share what they notice.)
 What's one true thing about the world that this photo shows?"
(Describe true things about the world, or about people. Share orally at first, then ask students to write them down.)
"Excellent! Let's put some of these around the room."

Step 3: Write truisms from prompts
"This time I'm not going to give you a truism or a picture. I'm going to put some plain words up. You look at the words and then make a two-minute drawing of whatever the words made you think of. Ready?"

(Write something on the overhead like "something exciting" or "something surprising" or something equally wide-open.)
"Read those words and draw whatever comes to mind. Even stick figures will be okay." *(Let two minutes pass.)*
"Now stop. Look at your picture the same way we looked at the photos on the wall. Think up a truism that you believe is true about the world or about people." *(Share and debrief.)*

Debriefing Questions:

1. If a statement is true to me, is it going to be true for everyone?

2. The truisms that you wrote are so much better than the original statement with the photograph. Do you agree? How do you explain that? How can you tell they're better?

3. If everyone used the same prompt, would their essays all be very similar?

4. Would most people's essays be almost the same if everyone used their own truism?

5. Once you have a truism you really like, and you want to use it to write your essay, what might be your next step?

Spin-offs:

1. Reteach: Some student-written truisms will not be truisms, but will be about specific people or incidents. Refine the concept by reading a series of sentences, and after each ask, "Is this about one person? Or all people?" Examples: *I have a friend named Joe.* (That's not a truism about all people in general.) *Kids need friends.* (That's a truism; it's true about all people in general.) *The boy likes his friend.* (That's not a truism; it's not true about all people in general.) *Friends can make you crazy.* (That's a truism; it's true about all people in general.)

2. Talk through the students' truisms, allowing them to tell how they know the truisms are true. This is a great rehearsal for essay-writing.

3. Write an essay using a truism as the central idea.

4. After having read a piece of literature, let students write a truism and find a graphic to go with it and with the literature. Then ask them to write what that truism and graphic have to do with the piece of literature, or why they chose it. This is a wonderful, kid-friendly way to teach literary analysis. See the sample below.

Student Samples:

Truisms by twelfth graders from discussions without photographs
(contributed by students in Dottie Hall's English 4 classes):

Students were in groups based on their summer reading, which was in the biography/autobiography genre. There was an athlete group, a movie star group, a historical figures group, an artist group. At the beginning of the grouping they went around the circle and told who their person was and then talked about three interesting/amazing things they learned about that person. They took all of those and drew conclusions that turned into the truisms. So the truisms were collaborative.

1. In life's struggles, perseverance is the key.
2. Being in the public eye opens you up to criticism.
3. The actions of the past become the hands that mold the present.
4. Parents give us life but inspiration gives us the fuel to live.
5. Faith gives us the strength to stand up for what we believe in.
6. Illness can be your biggest competitor.
7. Criticism can weaken or strengthen a person's beliefs.
8. It's important to always remember where you came from.
9. Artists have nonverbal ways of expressing themselves.
10. Fame isn't always as glamorous as it seems.
11. Beauty is power.
12. The past can have many haunting truths.
13. The love for fame reduces the love for others.
14. To get to the top of the ladder, you must start on the bottom rung.
15. The stress of fame is equal to the ease of normality.
16. Love can be deadly.
17. All work and no play can make a person *insane*.

Photo by Gretchen Bernabei

136. People create their own punishments.
La gente crea sus propios castigos.

Truisms by fourth graders from looking only at the photo:

The future is locked until its moment. —Wesley

Everyone has a secret. —Brandon

Even something so small can make a big difference. —Sallie

Small things can hold everything together. —Lindsey

If you do drugs, you'll get locked-up. —Donald

There's always a key in life. —Jessica

Everyone gets in trouble. —Brandy

Some things can't be opened. —Victor

Not everything is unlocked for you. —Joel

The truth will set you free. —Jevon

Not everything's easy to get through. —Roxanne

Unlock your freedom. —Derek

You have to work to find the key to life. —Hillary

Some things are best sealed up. —Etan

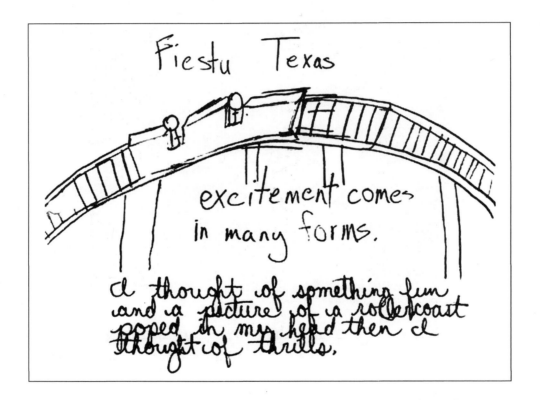

A fourth grader looked at the prompt, "Life has all kinds of adventure." Next, she drew the picture. Then, looking only at her drawing, she thought of a truism: "Excitement comes in many forms." This sample demonstrates that students can come up with better prompts by looking at graphics, even rough graphics that they themselves produce. Sketching a picture, therefore, can be an important step for unity and focus, in between reading a prompt and beginning to write.

This fourth grader copied the prompt, "Life has all kinds of adventures." He then sketched the first drawing that came to his mind, a classroom scene in which he and a friend were exchanging notes, and everyone told the teacher. Looking at his drawing brought him to a new truism, "Life has challenges." His teacher asked him to try to come up with three potential truisms or titles, and he added, "Trying to get around," and "I wish we never had hands." Clearly, his story about the perceived betrayal of his classmates as an example of challenges in life would answer the original prompt, but with a personal, authentic, and engaging spin of his very own.

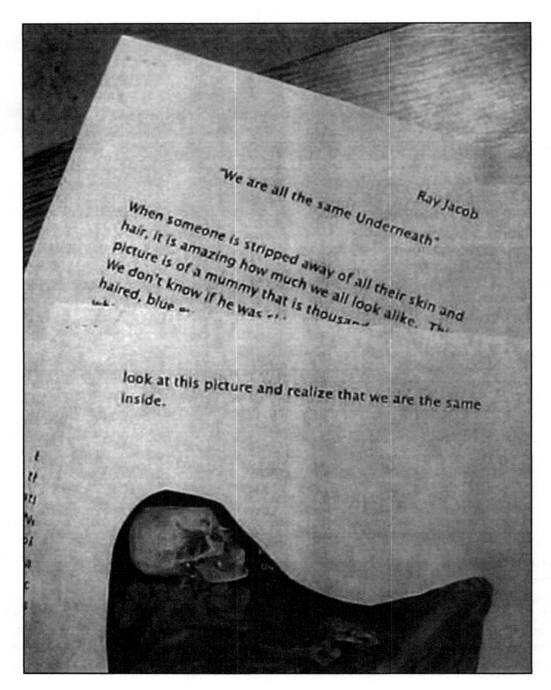

"We are all the same Underneath"

Ray Jacob

When someone is stripped away of all their skin and hair, it is amazing how much we all look alike. Th... picture is of a mummy that is thousan... We don't know if he was... haired, blue...

look at this picture and realize that we are the same inside.

After reading *Roll of Thunder, Hear My Cry*, sixth-grade students of Suzi Lockamy found a graphic that they thought related to the book and wrote a truism to go with it. Their real thinking showed when she asked them to explain in an essay how they chose that truism and that graphic, and how they related to the book.

Full Essay by fourth grader about life's adventures:

Splash! Someone had sprayed our windows with a hose. Bobby, our sister Jenny's "karate dude" boyfriend, looked out the window. It was 8:07 p.m. Our parents were at work, and Owen & Tim went to a restaurant. (Owen is our other sister and Tim is her "military kick-butt" fiancé.) Maybe Owen & Tim are back, I thought. Jenny was probably thinking the same because she called Owen's cell phone. She looked nervous when she announced that Owen said she was picking up Tim's boxes right now.

Bobby was having a hard time seeing what was outside because every time he tried to look, the water splashed the window again. He and Jenny mumbled to each other. They led Frankie (my brother) and me to a bathroom where they told us to stay until they came back. I realized that they were checking for thieves or vandalizers and wanted us to be safe.

When they came back they rushed us outside in the cool night air and into Bobby's jeep. While we buckled our seatbelts I whispered to Frankie what I thought was going on. We both broke down crying because we were so scared. Jenny was frozen in her seat, and Bobby was doing his best to comfort us as he drove us around the neighborhood. I kept on picturing our house on fire while the silhouettes of drunk vandalizers laughed. "How can this happen to us? Nothing this bad ever happened." I thought. Frankie was squeezing me so tight I felt like I was going to pop.

Bobby was driving down a route that Frankie and I knew led to our house. "No Bobby, don't go there please! Don't go there!" Frankie and I begged. He just kept on driving.

When I saw the light on our porch on, I thought, "They are in the house. Lord, the robbers are in the house." I started sobbing hysterically. Frankie didn't though. In fact as soon as the jeep stopped, he ran out and hugged 2 figures at the door. Jenny came out with Bobby. I wouldn't come out though. I squished myself into a corner and Bobby had to carry me into the house. When I realized who the 2 figures were I was so mad and embarrassed that I yelled and tried to hit them.

They explained to Jenny and I that they were picking up boxes in the backyard. They said that they weren't trying to play a trick, they were just trying to get our attention. They were no other than Owen and Tim.

    - Frances Imperial, grade 4

For classroom duplication only. Enlarge at 121% for 81/2 x 11 sheet

Lesson 2:
Prompt Generator

When a class is reading a piece of literature, the "literary essay" can become daunting. How do we guide students toward a point in their essay? Some teachers think up a topic for discussion in an essay, commonly a theme found in the literature. Some teachers find essay assignments in ancillary materials provided by publishers. Sometimes students are given unfettered freedom to come up with their own topics, with less-than-stellar results ("There is lots of ambition in Macbeth").

The problem is that students need a meaningful topic for writing. And it can be tricky, convincing students to tie personal meaning to the literature they've read. A handy solution was developed by teachers Kristy Truss and Cyndi Pina. In this easy group or individual activity, students have a concrete, step-by-step method to generate their own focused topics from a piece of literature.

Teaching It:

You are focusing on one piece of literature (for example, Macbeth). What is this story mostly about? On the left side of your paper, make a list of five or six of the main issues that this book/story is about.
(Demonstrate a starter for the group.)
Macbeth, for example, is about greed . . . and what else? Yes! Ambition . . . about marriage . . . There are no wrong answers. (Pause.)
Now draw a grid on your paper like this:

	Good	Bad
Greed		
Ambition		
Morals		

In the next columns, think up and write down one good thing about greed.
(Demonstrate: "Greed can . . . get you moving.")
And in the next column, think up and write down one bad thing about greed.
(Demonstrate: "Greed . . . yes! Can destroy your health.")
Everyone clear? See if you can finish these.
(Share, compile, and publish on the wall or in typed-up list form.)

Debriefing Questions:

1. Was this easy?

2. Why are these sentences more useful than typical textbook thematic prompts?

3. How could you combine sentences together to create more complex statements?

Spin-offs:

1. Instead of focusing on literature, ask students to list the most important things in the world to them.

2. Substitute words from the following list for "good" and "bad."

important

curious

silly

surprising

disappointing

paradoxical

sad

confusing

Student Samples

	Good	Bad
Greed	Greed keeps people interested in life.	Because of greed, the progression of the human race has slowed down.
Ambition	Ambition gives us will and helps us accomplish our goals.	Sometimes we have destructive ambitions, like to hurt someone.
Morals	Morals help guide us down a path of good choices.	Not enough people have morals.

Lesson 3:
Mixed Feelings: The 52/49 Split

Students aren't skilled at grappling with issues. They want to have a position instantly. An unwavering, strong, single position. Many students seem to consider the act of changing their minds equivalent to an act of weakness, or concession, or defeat. This way of viewing thinking is not only immature, it's also dangerous in a democracy where reasonable, informed voters make decisions for the nation. Consider the sayings that "becoming is more important than being," and "the journey is the destination." Likewise, the way an opinion is forming in a student's mind is more critical (and interesting) than what the opinion is.

In our world, we are commonly rewarded for confidence, for taking a stand, for knowing our minds. If someone throws out a topic, we can match their speed by throwing out an equally quick opinion about the topic. For or against. One hundred percent. No doubts.

In our hearts and minds, though, we might not be as sure as we sound. Students need to be guided to make use of the ambiguities they feel, and of the opinions they have that are still actually in formation. Newkirk reminds us that John Dewey valued an "attitude of suspended conclusion," which seems to signal a mind that is still taking in data and is willing to waver and change.

The following lesson, most useful with older students, uses two mentor texts that demonstrate the contemplative nature of forming opinions. The lesson helps to create a way of thinking that can have a huge impact on the way students grapple with the complexities that may be invisible but are nevertheless present in any writing prompt.

Teaching It:

Have you seen the Disney film *The Emperor's New Groove*? Do you remember how one of the characters had an angel on one shoulder and a devil on another? We all have something like that, conflicting voices in our heads, arguing over anything we have strong feelings about. We don't live in a simple world, and very little is all good or all bad. And if our writing isn't bogus writing, that struggle is in there somewhere. Let's read a couple of samples that show some internal grappling going on.

The first one is an excerpt from an NPR interview with Thomas Friedman, a foreign affairs columnist with *The New York Times* whose reporting on the Middle East won the Pulitzer Prize. *(Read the Friedman excerpt below.)*

Now, let's look at it again, and color-code the grappling. Pick two colors, and let's highlight/underline. Identify the two forces pushing and pulling the speaker. Underline all the words and phrases that reveal one feeling in one color and the other feeling with the other color. *(Read the Friedman excerpt again.)*
(Debrief about the nature of grappling in writing and in life.)

From an Interview with Thomas Friedman on the Post-Saddam Middle East

Mr. FRIEDMAN: ...for me, Terry...people would say, "What is your view on this war?" and I'd say "I'm for it 51/49." Actually what I told people, "I'm for it 52/49," because there are some things slightly irrational about my support for the war, and so it never really added up, and it was always for me a struggle between hope and experience. You know, Lord knows, experience from having lived in Lebanon—and what is Lebanon but just a small version of Beirut—should have taught me that the notion of nation-building and democratizing Iraq is a huge, huge project if not a fool's errand. You know, experience should have taught me that we just don't do these things very well. My wife was against the war, and when I wrote that in the column that, you know, I was leaning for it, my wife was against it, I was inundated with e-mail from people saying, "Listen to your wife. Your wife is smarter than you. I'm glad you sleep with someone more intelligent than you." And so it was always a struggle, but see, there was another side to it, and that was the hope side. I always say there's kind of two sides to my reporting. There's the Middle East side, and there's the Middle West side. There's the Minnesota boy and there's the reporter who went to Beirut, and they're constantly in a struggle for my soul. And the hope side really came from my travels since 9/11 and the number of young Arabs and Muslims who have come up to me in the Arab world and said, "Mr. Friedman, keep writing what you are writing. Keep calling for democracy. Keep calling for modernization in Islam." I've been bombarded with e-mail, particularly from Muslim women who have made that appeal. And so every time, Terry, that I thought of coming out against the war, it struck me as an abandonment of those people, which is why I just couldn't pull the trigger on it, and it's why hope always triumphed over experience, and why for me, it was always, you know, a 52/49 call.

Transcript Title: "INTERVIEW: THOMAS FRIEDMAN DISCUSSES POST-SADDAM MIDDLE EAST"
Excerpt used courtesy of *Fresh Air* with Terry Gross, produced in Philadelphia by WHYY.

For classroom duplication only. Enlarge at 121% for 81/2 x 11 sheet

Reviving The Essay © 2005 Discover Writing Press • www.discoverwriting.com   **13**

A Letter from the Austin American-Statesman

America's Freedoms

There is too much polarization and name-calling right now on what the media have simplistically labeled "pro" and "anti" war. I believe that most reasonable people have mixed feelings about this situation.

When I was 19, I found myself in Vietnam, while another kid I knew who was drafted went to Canada. I felt resentful at the time, but 30-plus years later, who was right and who was wrong has been lost in the turns of history. Few people said "welcome home" to either of us.

Then and now, I am thankful for the idealism and enthusiasm of young people. At this moment, a 19-year-old may be willingly risking life driving a tank in a desert, or may be carrying a peace sign in a town square. Each may be passionate and serious. Each may change their views many times over the next 30 years.

In the America that I fought for and believe in, I hope that reasonable people will be able to welcome them both home. In my America, public policy is formed by acting, speaking and voting one's conscience.

Terry Garity, Cedar Park
March 27, 2003

Spin-offs:

1. Find signs of grappling in a piece you wrote.

2. Rewrite the Friedman piece as a script, casting three characters as in *The Emperor's New Groove*.

3. Write about your opinions that have changed (sample below).

Things I Used to Hold a Firm Opinion About, But Now I Feel Differently About

by Veronica Marrero, grade 11

1. Chinese Food

   I never would have thought that I would like Chinese food. To me it looked nasty. Every time my family would go to a Chinese restaurant I would only eat the sweet and sour chicken. When I moved to DC there were carry-outs on every block. The carry-outs had Chinese food, hamburgers, fried chicken, sea food plates and hot wings. Since the carry out delivered to the base we had it like every night. I began to experiment and now I love Chinese food more than anything. Now that I live back in San Antonio its hard to find a Chinese restaurant as good as the carry-outs.

2. Punk Music and Tejano

   Living in DC all I listened to was rap and R&B. When I would turn on MTV and New Found People or Linkin Park came on I would change it. I wouldn't even try to listen to the words. When I first moved back to San Antonio, my cousin told me to listen to a song. After actually listening to the words, I fell in love with the song. A song by New Found Glory. The same with Tejano. After going to several Tejano festivals and a Tejano club, I now enjoy it, although I don't understand all the words.

3. Marriage and Children

   All my life I have said that I was not going to get married or have children. I would be a single business women. I certainly didn't want children because when I was around them I wanted to strangle them. Now, I think I have found someone that I can see myself settling down with and having children. I now realize that I don't have tolerance because the children are not my own. I'm sure that when I have my own, I'll be patient.

Lesson 4:
Prompt Roundup

Sometimes students have a general idea about their prompt, but they don't have a clue yet what to say about it. They haven't scratched through their accumulated experiences to arrive at a point they'd like to talk about, based on the prompt. Talking about it can help.

Talk is an often-overlooked part of the writing process, and a discussion can be a valid rehearsal for writing. We often ask students to do short writing exercises, or prewriting exercises like mind mapping or webbing, listing or freewriting, to uncover their thoughts. While these are all valid forms of response to a prompt, speaking and listening can be powerful ways to respond to a prompt as well.

How do we guide students to discuss topics? High school teacher Carol Siskovic has developed a "roundup" process which helps break down the discussion process into workable steps. It begins with a concrete set of questions (below) that students answer about the prompt. When they've finished answering their questions, they are ready to participate in a discussion.

Like the other lessons in this chapter, this activity provides students with one technique for figuring out "where to go" with a prompt, by thinking thoroughly about it before picking up a pen. This activity can be done in conjunction with other lessons in this chapter, or as a stand-alone.

Teaching It:

Students, today you're going to earn your grade by responding to a prompt. Your response will not be in the form of an essay, though, but in a roundup, or discussion. I'll show you the prompt, and you'll prepare your roundup questions so you'll be ready. *(Do. Give them ten or so minutes.)*

Let's go over the rules and roles of roundup.
(Go over some ground rules. Appoint leaders, arrange chairs into a circle, and let them discuss.)

Debriefing Questions:

1. What does talking have to do with writing?

2. Should you get a grade for participating in discussions?

3. What are some other ways that talk helps your writing processes?

Student _____ Prompt:_____

Saddle Ponderings for Roundup

1. **Paraphrase the statement that we are discussing, twice, using different words each time.**
   A.
   B.

2. **Which word or phrase do you find most interesting and why?**

3. **In a complete sentence of about a dozen words, explain how you know this statement is true.**

4. **Now, name at least two happenings in the real world (current or historical) that also illustrate how true the statement is.**
   A.
   B.

5. **List two "how or why" questions about the statement under discussion that needs team consideration and clarification. Be ready with some possible answers.**
   A.
   B.

6. **Can you think of any song(s) that are related to the statement? Write down some snippets of lyrics to any songs you can think of.**

7. **Think of a personal association with the statement, something or someone from your own experience brought to mind. Explain. Be specific, not general.**

8. **Think of a literary association with this work under discussion—name a specific book, story, poem, play, TV program, movie, or any creative composition. Explain their similarities.**

9. **Can you think of an opposite yet true version of this statement? Write it below.**

10. **Evaluate the statement in some manner (1 to 4 stars, jalapeños, etc.) Explain.**

11. **Compose and design a T-shirt (front and back) for this statement. Use class-appropriate artwork or words. Remember to brand the shirt somewhere with author and title of work. Be creative.**

Front

Back

For classroom duplication only. Enlarge at 121% for 81/2 x 11 sheet

2

Finding (or Inventing) Your Structure

How to Use Text Structures

We all know the structure that Tom Romano calls "the five-paragraph you-know-what." You tell them what you're going to tell them (in paragraph one), then tell them (in paragraphs two, three, and four), then tell them what you told them (in paragraph five). This structure provides one way to turn a blank page into a page with some writing on it, but it has produced generations of flat, formulaic pieces. But if we throw out the formula five-paragraph essay, what do we use instead? Everyone knows that students need something to start with.

Perhaps it would help to return to the purpose of essays. In his *Critical Thinking and Writing: Reclaiming the Essay*, Thomas Newkirk writes:

> *If writing is to be a "unique mode of thinking," we should ask how writing can foster and track movement of the mind.*

How do we teach students to "track the movement of their minds"? How do we teach structure without formula? Do we make new roadmaps? This chapter explores alternative text structures, as well as ways to use the structures with students.

In order for students to do any of these lessons, they first have to have a prompt. Maybe it's an actual test prompt, telling them something like "Write about a day when something unbelievable happened." Maybe it's a pithy quotation from Bartlett's. Maybe it's a student-written truism about people, about human nature, about the world. Maybe it's a theme from a piece of literature. Any of these would serve as prompts to be developed through the text structures.

Once students have a prompt they believe, you have some choices about how much direction to give students. These ideas guide me:

1. Students sometimes need freedom to discover and invent new structures.

2. Students sometimes need leadership in directed, guided writing.

3. The goal is to give students a range of choices, rather than one rigid formula.

4. Whatever works, is right.

So it makes sense to let students experiment, sometimes freewriting with prompts and discovering text structures within their freewriting, and sometimes working with text structure models, collecting structures that work to add to their repertoire. As they practice additional structures, it takes fewer repetitions for students to internalize the steps. Ultimately, they become readers in search of new structures to imitate. Therefore, the structures listed here are a beginning list, and with your students, you will build a list that surpasses this one as you add their inventions and "found" structures from their reading.

The goal of these structures is to supply organizational patterns while giving students a means to trace the movement of their thoughts. Once students have converted the movement of their thoughts into prose form, they have a draft. Then they can rearrange their text pieces into whatever order they'd like to present it to a reader, deciding what should go first, what to end with, how to have the thoughts unfold.

And if we need permission to have students play with forms like this, Frank Smith gives it to us in *Essays into Literacy*:

> *Myth: Writing is a linear, left-to-right process.*
>
> *Reality: Writing can be done in several places and directions concurrently and is as easily manipulated in space as it is in time. Texts can be constructed from writing done on separate pieces of paper, in notebooks, on index cards or on chalkboards, at the same time that a main draft is being produced. Words and lines can be moved around on a page just as pages themselves can be reshuffled into different sequences.*
>
> *Writing is a plastic art. (83)*

Teaching Variations, Using Prompts

It's best to use variety in class, and to give students many different experiences with their writing. Some students need more guidance; some feel constrained by guidance. Regardless, all of the following approaches are useful for just about everyone. It's helpful to rotate through these options, depending on which would fit best for your needs. Once you see signs of doldrums from students, pop in some variety.

Samples of all of these options are included throughout this chapter.

Option 1: Freewriting

The students write for several minutes, looking at a photo, or thinking about a prompt, or ruminating on a word in the prompt. Then they do some reading aloud of the results, to see what developed. This is a little like shrimping, with a net that you haul up every once in a while to see what all got in there. Sometimes it doesn't smell very good, but sometimes you'll find a treasure.

Option 2: Timed, Guided Writing

One form of timed, guided writing is the cubing activity developed by Elizabeth Cowan. The teacher prompts the students with one question about the subject, and the students write for just a few minutes; she stops them, asks them a different question and they write again; these steps are repeated six times for cubing. The students all stay on the same step, with the teacher stopping and starting them.

These steps can be done on one paper, indenting for each new step, or on separate index cards, to be shuffled and reordered at the writer's will.

Will students remember the structure on their own? Will the structure become a tool in the students' arsenal of choices? With practice, yes. One try at a structure isn't enough for it to become the students' own, to become internalized. With high school freshmen, I generally use the first structure on five different days, with five different prompts. By about the fifth day, they need little reminding of the steps.

Option 3: Kernel Essays

Students write their prompt at the top of the page. Below it, they choose (or create) a text structure and draw the boxes. Below that, they write one sentence for each box in the text structure. When they read these sentences aloud to a listener, it's easy to tell whether they hang together cohesively. So then any part of this could be expanded into an essay. Or not. Just doing the kernel essay is a useful exercise.

Lesson 5:
The Insight Garden: Growing Opinions from Art, Literature, and Life

---

Insight Garden

An insight about life	One illustration from literature	One illustration from a movie	An illustration from my life	I wonder

---

This structure is like mental gymnastics: students take the prompt and find evidence of it in three different media: literature, movies, and their life experience. In essence, it asks students to have a conversation with themselves about where else they've seen that thought in action. The ending guides them to listen to their own discussion and uncover a question that their conversation leads them to ask. A conclusion like this furthers the discussion instead of repeating the starting point, which adds to the reader's sense of interest in the resulting piece.

Regardless of the exercise, this kind of structure will work best if the prompt is accompanied by a photograph or piece of artwork, which seems to unlock for students their inner "knowing" about the thought in the prompt.

Teaching *The Insight Garden* as a Timed, Guided Writing:

(On an overhead projector, place a piece of artwork and an opinion or theme statement that correlates with a piece of literature you are reading in class. This guided writing will take eleven minutes.)

1. Look at the artwork.

2. Copy the statement.

3. For the next minute, explain the statement. (What does it mean? What is your interpretation of it?)

4. Take a breath and indent. For the next three minutes, tell how it's true in a piece of literature, a story.

5. Take a breath and indent. For the next three minutes, tell how it's true in a movie you've seen.

6. Take a breath and indent. For the next three minutes, tell how it connects to your life, our world.

7. Take a breath and indent one more time. In the next minute, finish with something your discussion leaves you wondering about the statement.
(Share, either with partners or in large group, using volunteers.)
(Discuss any of the following.)
Did looking at the artwork change the way you started writing?
How difficult was it to connect the idea to literature? A movie? Your life?
What would you need to do to lead the paragraphs from one to the next?
Are you surprised at how much you wrote in eleven minutes?

Teaching *The Insight Garden* as a Kernel Essay:

(On an overhead projector, place a piece of artwork and an opinion or theme statement that correlates with a piece of literature you are reading in class, like the sample shown.)

1. Take a look at the sentence and the artwork, students. *(Read the statement aloud.)* Do you agree with it? If you do, copy it at the top of your page. Do you need to change some of the words to make it more true for you? If you do, go ahead and revise the sentence, and doing that will make it a prompt that you believe is true. Write your version at the top of your page. *(On the blackboard or overhead, display the text structure boxes shown at the beginning of this lesson.)*

2. Directly underneath the statement, copy these boxes, including the words in them.

3. Now on your paper, underneath the boxes, write one sentence to go with each of the boxes. If you'd like to draw a line from your sentence to the box, go ahead. You have about five minutes. You've already got your sentence for the first box. *(Give the students writing time.) (Share, either with partners or in large group, using volunteers.)*

4. Do the sentences all "hang together"? *(Discuss the cohesiveness or need for transitions.)*

5. Was this hard or easy? *(Discuss why.)*

6. Do you hear how each one of those kernel essays is just like a perfect plan for a whole essay? How any one of them could be expanded into a full-blown, wonderful essay? *(Decide with the class what to do with the essays next, whether to work on them or abandon them and move on.)*

The "Insight Garden" first appeared as Lesson 23 in Barry Lane and Gretchen Bernabei's book, *Why We Must Run with Scissors: Voice Lessons in Persuasive Writing* (Shoreham, VT: Discover Writing Press, 2001).

Photo by Terry Moore

074. When you fall in love, you're willing to look more foolish than at any other time in your life.

Cuando te enamoras no te importa hacer tonterías que jamás hubieras hecho.

Truism Samples

Sometimes appearances can make you misjudge someone. —Susan

Nobody can teach someone how to grow up. —David

Every group has one weak link. —Sean

Guided Writing Sample

Foolish Love
Pamela Edge, Teacher

When you fall in love, you are willing to look more foolish than at any other time in your life. Perhaps, it was my immaturity. Perhaps, it was true love. Perhaps, it was flat out the stupidest thing I have ever done.

My semi-tragic love story reminds me of the children's book, *The Frog Prince*. In this epic love story, the princess kisses a frog. After a blast of bright lights and romantic music, the frog transforms from a slimy creature to a ravishing prince. In my love story, I would have done anything including, but not limited to, diving into a leech infested pond of green scum just to place a lip lock on my frog of a prince, Andrew.

Of course, my actions could have landed me with the starring role in the next *Revenge of the Nerds* movie. However, with my love-stricken actions, the movie producers would have to change the movie title to *Revenge of the Love Seeking Nerd*. This title change encompasses the raw powers of emotions only love at the most infant stage can bring.

In all the movies and books about damsels trying to woo her love, pain seems to be the most common thread. Whether it was lovesickness resulting in pain, a woman about to be in pain, or the damsel who was a pain, the true love story always involved pain. My master plan was to apprehend Andrew's love by forcing him to save me from a threatening, possibly painful, situation. So, I climbed up in a tree and hung upside down. Hey, I was only 9. Taking a deep breath, I screamed and hollered until I sounded like a bull frog, but Frog Prince never jumped to save me.

Now at 30 something, I have always wondered why? Why didn't Andrew ever notice me? Was it my looks? Did he not like my tree climbing? Or was it the fact I could not sway Andrew's focus away from baseball, basketball, or swimming in a leech-infested pond?

Kernel Essay Sample

Sometimes appearances can make you judge someone before you even get to know that person.

In Julius Caesar, Brutus acted and pretended to be Caesar's friend.

Hitler never showed how prejudice he was against the Jews until he was in power.

I had a friend who lied about everything, always saying how rich she was and how she had the perfect family.

I think that nobody is completely honest with their appearance; I do, though, wonder what if everybody was honest and showed their appearance.

—Lucia, grade 10

Lesson 6:
A Memory

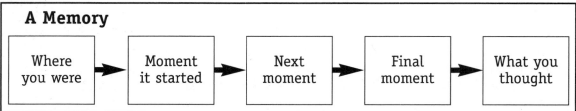

A Memory

Where you were → Moment it started → Next moment → Final moment → What you thought

The events in our lives give us most of our knowledge. Furthermore, nothing is more powerful to a reader than story. So clearly, a great way to convey an idea, or respond to a prompt, is through the form of a narrative, and one simple way to handle this is by telling a clear, focused memory.

Teaching *A Memory* as a Timed, Guided Writing:

(On an overhead projector, place a piece of artwork and an opinion or theme statement that correlates with a piece of literature you are reading in class, like the sample: Even sad things are important.*) This guided writing will take eleven minutes.*

1. Look at the artwork as I read the statement to you. *(Read it aloud.)*
2. Now think about your life as I read the statement again. *(Read it aloud again.)*
3. Has anything ever happened in your life that would make you say this statement? Does the statement remind you about something that happened to you?
   In the next minute, tell where you were when that incident happened. If you can't think of anything, keep looking at the picture.
4. Take a breath and indent. For the next two minutes, tell what happened when the memory began.
5. Take a breath and indent. For the next two minutes, tell what happened next.
6. Take a breath and indent. For the next two minutes, tell what happened last.
7. Take a breath and indent one more time. In the next minute, finish with what you thought, what you said to yourself, after that last moment.

(Share, either with partners or in large group, using volunteers.)
(Discuss any of the following.)
How quickly did you think of an incident that happened?
What made you think of it more, the picture, or the words?
Was it easy to tell each moment in two minutes?
Did anyone have trouble telling what happened in the next moments? Why?

Teaching *A Memory* as a Kernel Essay:

(On an overhead projector, place a piece of artwork and an opinion or theme statement that correlates with a piece of literature you are reading in class.)

1. Take a look at the sentence and the artwork, students. *(Read the statement aloud. Sample:* **Even sad things can be important.***)* Do you agree with it? If you do, copy it at the top of your page. Do you need to change some of the words to make it more true for you? If you do, go ahead and revise the sentence, and doing that will make it a prompt that you believe is true. Write your version at the top of your page.

(On the blackboard or overhead, display the text structure boxes shown at the beginning of this lesson.)

2. Directly underneath the statement, copy these boxes, including the words in them.

3. Now on your paper, underneath the boxes, write one sentence to go with each of the boxes. If you'd like to draw a line from your sentence to the box, go ahead. You have about five minutes. Maybe you've already got your sentence for the last box. *(Give the students writing time.)*

(Share either with partners or in large group, using volunteers.)

4. Do the sentences all "hang together"? *(Discuss the cohesiveness or need for transitions.)*

5. Was this hard or easy? *(Discuss why.)*

6. Do you hear how each one of those kernel essays is just like a perfect plan for a whole essay? How any one of them could be expanded into a full-blown, wonderful essay? *(Decide with the class what to do with the essays next, whether to work on them or abandon them and move on.)*

One day at school I got four write ups. I was furious. They even stapled a note on my shirt. On the way out, I thought about throwing the note in the trash. But I think the janitor might see it, no it's too risky, I burn the house down.

I walked to my house. I thought about it as I walked home, it is possible if I plan it right. I saw my friend Rosco, he asked me if I could play.

Then, he saw my note from the teacher. He carefully read the note. After he read the note he told me that I was in big trouble. We walked to my house and I told him my plan. I sneaked through the back door of my house. I felt like I was James Bond. I tiptoed from the hallway to the bathroom. I opened the drawers, and took out my dad's cigar lighter. I yanked the note off me and lit the note on fire. The next thing that happened was bad luck. My toothbrush fell in the fire. Sssssssssss! It made a funny smell. Just then my Dad walked in and asked me "What is that smell?" He noticed me burning the note and quickly stomped out the note. He ran to get a belt. I knew I was in trouble.

—Traevon Taylor, grade 4

Photo by Matilde Bernabei

003. Even sad things are important.
Hasta las cosas tristes son importantes.

Truism Samples

Sometimes people need a dog to comfort them. —Alex, grade 11

Dogs can keep secrets. —Henry, grade 4

Dogs speak human. —Matilde, grade 8

Freewriting Samples

Even Sad Things can be Important

My Krissy (dog Kris) passed away of kidney failure in June. Even though he was sixteen human years old (112 in dog years) and we knew he was going to pass away we did not want to let him go. He did not pass away like most dogs do; we had to have him put him to sleep. My mom had him ever since he was a pup and she could not put him to sleep so my dad and grandpa took him to the vet. My dad had to dig Kris' grave by himself. He made a cross to put on his grave that said 'God Bless—You Will Be Missed.' We were so sad and depressed for three weeks. On July 4 my mom put a little flag on the grave because he was her 'Little Hero.' Today we like to go back there where his grave is. My last memory of him is the morning he passed on and we took a picture. I really miss my dog. We will not get a dog for a long time because nothing can fill the emptiness in our hearts where he was and still is.
—Suzanne Thayer, grade 4
Student of Catherine Ramirez
Round Rock ISD

I think even sad things are important because if someone or something dies then it would be sad but it would also be an important part of your life. I've had to deal with my grandma and grandpa dying and it was very important, but also very hard to get over the sadness and devastation. I know that they are gone forever and someday I will be dead also.
—Kevin Hunt, grade 9

"Zach, Alex is dead!" Hearing those words was one of the saddest moments of my life. It was also one of the most important things in my life. His death is so important to me that I have to keep a damn laminated newspaper clipping and picture of him. His death was just the slap in the face I needed: to take life as it is and not waste your time to give a flying flip about what others care. My sadness from his death will never end. It's an endless sea, a bottomless hole where my heart lies.
—Zach Durden, grade 9

Guided Writing Samples

Better off Doing Things Alone

One night, my supposed-to-be friend, Javier, and I were on the way to a school dance when I guess I said something to make him mad enough to hit like a moron.

The next thing I know he had already hit me with a lock twice. I told him, "You must be retarded to hit me like that." I was stunned for a minute, but when I realized what happened I just snapped like a pit bull.

I remember that they didn't even take him to jail for assault. I told the cop I didn't do anything here except defend myself. The cops decided to take me instead. I have the guarantee that I will never have to hear from that guy again.

Thanks to him I will never be able to trust anyone like I did before that night happened. To all my audiences who read this story, on a piece of my life, this made me who I am today. Some people can get you in trouble and that is why it's better to stand alone.
—Joe Uresti, grade 11

Kernel Essay Samples

Better Place

Around seven or eight years ago, my favorite uncle passed away by a drive by shooting in Los Angeles, California. My mom sat me down and started to talk to me about the way of life and how it works.

From that day on, I understood that dying was just a part of life and everyone that I love will soon pass away too.

Mom made us move from home to Texas, so my dad could get his mind off things and try to start a new life.
—Sandra Sotero, grade 12

A Man Who Lived a Miracle
Jenny Jenkins, 7th grade

On October 18, 2002, I watched him lie there on the football field; people ran frantically to help. I sat on the cold bleachers watching his every step. Each step he began to become weaker, falling like he was drunk. A doctor came to examine him but every moment he began to fall over like he was about to fall asleep. Then the helicopter came and in a flash, he was gone. As my feet swiftly moved from the cold bleachers to the steel chairs in the waiting room, I was thinking all at once.

Is he ok?

Is it serious?

I felt scared thinking he was going to die.

It all passed in a blur the cheering of the people faded away to the silence of tears; the smell of popcorn and refreshments in the air changed to gross hospital food. Waiting among other people while sitting in steel, cold chairs I see my dad come out to these two double doors. He explains to us the trauma of what happened and what the doctor quoted. For the first time in my life, I saw tears running down my dad's cheeks. Each tear filled with sorrow and his smiled changed to trembling lips.

With disbelief that all this happened, my aunt took me to her house to stay the night. I cried myself to sleep to get away from the nightmare.

The next morning I woke up with dried tears all over my face. My parents came to pick me up that afternoon to bring me home.

I asked, "Mom, do you think he is all right?"

She answered almost trying to whisper, "I am not sure sweetie. They put him in intensive care."

"Can I see him," I asked.

"I'm sorry, but you are too young," she replied. "You must be thirteen".

With a tear rolling down my cheek I said, "Okay."

For the next few days, I had troubles falling asleep without crying. I kept thinking to myself, when would I get to see him?

I asked, "Daddy will I ever get to see him?"

He replied, "I am not sure."

My Dad finally made the decision to sneak me in. For that one moment, I was filled with happiness.

The next morning we arrived at the hospital I felt as anxious as a jackrabbit. I walked in the room that Matt was staying in. For the first time in like forever, well at least it seemed like it, I got to see my brother's face. He looked different lying there in a hospital bed. He gave me a smile but only one side of his mouth came up because he was still recovering the other side, which lost feeling. Within one day, Matt moved to a regular room.

On October 25, 2002, doctors released Matthew Charles Jenkins from the university hospital. He took physical therapy a few weeks after. His recovery was rapid. He successfully turned out normal through the entire trauma and lived a miracle.

I used to think he is going to die; there is no such way he can live. All I knew is that I could pray. Now I know that miracles truly do happen.

Prayers may bring answers but faith brings miracles.

For classroom duplication only. Enlarge at 121% for 81/2 x 11 sheet

Reviving The Essay © 2005 Discover Writing Press • www.discoverwriting.com

31

A Colorized Memory

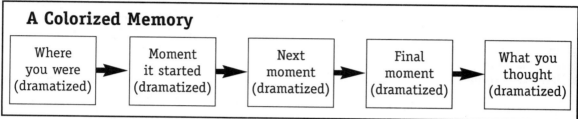

A Colorized Memory

| Where you were (dramatized) | → | Moment it started (dramatized) | → | Next moment (dramatized) | → | Final moment (dramatized) | → | What you thought (dramatized) |

Have you ever seen a movie that was made as a black-and-white film, and then colorized? The colors change the original film, sometimes making it look almost circus-like and bizarre. Sometimes writers begin with fact and depart from it in almost the same way, creating something interesting and fresh. Students often need permission to fictionalize something that seems mundane to them. This structure uses the same form as the memory structure, with a twist.

Teaching *A Colorized Memory* as a Timed, Guided Writing:

(On an overhead projector, place a piece of artwork and an opinion or theme statement that correlates with a piece of literature you are reading in class, like the sample given.)

1. Look at the artwork as I read the statement to you. (*Read it aloud. Sample:* Full trust can never exist between people.)
2. Now think about your life as I read the statement again. (*Read it aloud again.*)
3. Has anything ever happened in your life that would make you say this statement? In the next minute, tell where you were when that incident happened. If you can't think of anything, keep looking at the picture.
4. Take a breath and indent. For the next two minutes, tell how it all started.
5. Take a breath and indent. For the next two minutes, tell what happened in the next moment.
6. Take a breath and indent. For the next two minutes, tell what happened last.
7. Take a breath and indent one more time. In the next minute, finish with what you thought, what you said to yourself, after that last moment.
8. Now go back to each part, and liven it up by adding Hollywood movie details, details that are larger-than-life, or exaggerated.

(Share either with partners or in large group, using volunteers.)

(Discuss any of the following.)
What did you add to liven it up?
Was it easy, adding larger-than-life details?
Do you think a reader would like the story more now, with the new details?
Would it be easier to colorize as you go than to add the color as the last step?

Teaching *A Colorized Memory* as a Kernel Essay:

(On an overhead projector, place a piece of artwork and an opinion or theme statement that correlates with a piece of literature you are reading in class.)

1. Read the statement with me. (*Sample:* Full trust can never exist between people.)
2. Think of a memory, a moment that comes to mind. What if Hollywood moviemakers took your memory and turned it into a movie? It would have sensationalized details that didn't really happen at all, just to make the movie sell.
   (On the blackboard or overhead, display the text structure boxes shown at the beginning of this lesson.)
3. Directly underneath the statement, copy these boxes, including the words in them. Now on your paper, underneath the boxes, write one sentence to go with each of the boxes. If you'd like to draw a line from your sentence to the box, go ahead. You have about five minutes. You might already have your sentence for the last box. *(Give the students writing time.)*

(Share, either with partners or in large group, using volunteers.)
Are there any moments you could expand? *(Discuss the cohesiveness or need for transitions.)*
Was this hard or easy? *(Discuss why.)*
Do you hear how each one of those kernel essays is just like a perfect plan for a whole story? How any one of them could be expanded into a full-blown, wonderful essay? *(Decide with the class what to do with the essays next, whether to work on them or abandon them and move on.)*

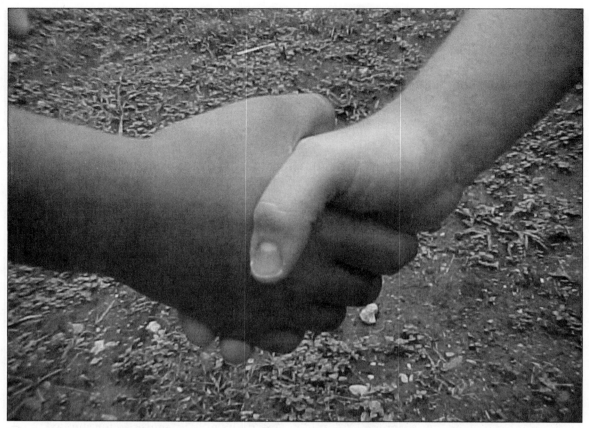
Photo by Gretchen Bernabei

209. Full trust can never exist between people.
Jamás existe completa confianza entre la gente.

Truism Samples

You've got to take chances. —Hillary

Not everyone's afraid. —Kevin

People need each other. —Kim

Guided Writing Samples

One Lie Changed my Life

Have you ever been lied to by your school principal? I know you are probably thinking that won't ever happen, but you are wrong because it happened to me.

It all began when I was in elementary school living with my grandmother. The whole day in school I felt like something horrible was going to happen. I went through the whole day feeling worried. I was just beginning to think that I was just being paranoid, when I was called in by the principal. I looked at the clock and it was 2:50, and I remember thinking that it was odd for the principal to be calling me in so late. I knew I wasn't trouble because I had not caused any trouble all day.

So when I arrived in the principal's office I immediately asked, "What have I done?" She told me I hadn't done anything. From the corner of my eye I saw my two younger brothers sitting down. I asked the principal, "Why are my brothers in here?" She told me that my grandmother was coming to pick us up. We knew that my grandmother never came to pick us up. My brother Adrian (the middle brother) gave me a look and we ran out of the office. Kevin (the youngest) just stayed seated and watched us run. When Adrian and I reached the last door we were caught by two police officers. We tried to get free, but we were overpowered. The two officers hand cuffed us and put us in the police vehicle. A social worker came and put Kevin in his car.

We were taken to a placement home called Boysville. My brother, Adrian, and I were constantly causing trouble, so they kicked us out. My brother Kevin did well, so he got to stay. Adrian and I were only there for two months.

Adrian and I were then sent to Laurel Ridge for two weeks. After those two weeks we were sent to another placement home called Southwest Center. We were there for six months. Adrian and I were then sent to another placement home called Baptist Children's Home. This is where we met the two most amazing people who changed our lives. Their names were Ann and John Bow and they are now my parents.

We have been adopted for six years now. But I consider them to be, and tell people that they are my biological parents. I truly believe that from this one lie I have been blessed to have two great parents and am now able to live a worry free life. I can also say that I know how it feels to have a family who love you so much that they would do anything for you. Before I was adopted, I didn't have a family who really cared for me. I owe my life to my parents and god for giving me a second chance to have a real family and be loved for who I am.

In a way, this lie was like a seed that my life sprouted from.

Alfred Bow, grade 11

Kernel Essay Samples

The Art of Deceit

I snuck into my house in the morning, the night after "spending the night at my friend's house," and slowly tried to creep into my bedroom to avoid detection. My parents began to question me. I lied more than once to get the questions coming from my parents to subside and get the moment over with. The play worked, but afterwards I felt bad because my parents probably just wanted the truth.

—Jonathan Martinez, grade 11

Full Essay Samples

River Panic
Bryce Turner, grade 4

I was in the log house putting on my swim suit for the tube ride. I got the sunscreen out and put it on as fast as lightning. I went outside to get my tube and started running. "Wait Bryce, we're not ready yet," Dad gushed. I waited for five minutes for them to get ready. Finally we headed for the river. The rocks were slippery and I kept on falling. I put my tube in the river and we were off.

We were coming up to this current. "I'm coming," I yelled. I went so fast that the current pushed me into a wall. Whew, I was ready for more. One hour later I had a problem. "Mom, I got to go," I said. "What do you mean go," Mom quoted. "You know, go," I quoted back. "Oh," Mom gushed, "then just go right now." "Now." "Okay." Then I just went. I was embarrassed.

Suddenly, I heard something. I looked around, but when I turned back Mom and Dad were gone. There was a waterfall coming. I shrieked in horror. I tried to turn back but it was no use. "Help," I yelled. Before I knew it I went down. My life jacket got stuck on a stick. I started to choke. I tried to say help but my mouth was full of water and nobody could hear me under 1,000,000 gallons of water. I started to turn red then blue. Then purple. I thought to myself that I was doomed. Then something grabbed my leg. Oh no, I thought, somebody is going to take me. When the stranger pulled me out, it was Dad.

We came up to a rough current and a smooth current. "We're going to the smooth current," Mom announced. Dad said that Bryce and me were going on the other one. That's not what I had in mind though. We started to go fast. Then there was a stick coming up. Oh no, my tube is going to pop, I thought. Dad grabbed my tube and pulled me to safety. Then we exited and crashed into Mom.

We were almost to the end. We stopped by the ledge and pulled ourselves out. "What a ride." I quoted. "You bet," Dad quoted back. Papa drove up with in his four wheeler. Papa brought some towels for us to dry off and sit on in the truck. I was shivering a lot. I'll never forget this day I thought.

Moral: Don't try things that are dangerous.

As a tradition in a lot of American families, on Easter the "Easter Bunny" would come and lay plastic eggs around the yard and in the eggs were little pieces of candy. In my family, all 18 of us would get together at our lake house at Medina Lake and there would be tons of eggs. All the other grandkids and I would run around for hours trying to find the eggs.

I can't remember what age I was, but when my older cousins reached their teenage years, they got less and less interested in collecting the eggs and getting the candy, but more and more interested in hiding the eggs in places where nobody could find them. There was a method to their madness; because my little brother was a diabetic, we filled half of the eggs with money. The only eggs they would hide in these places were the ones with money. After everyone was asleep, they would go out and collect the eggs with the money in them, then put all the money in a stash in their bedroom at the lake house. After a few years the stash built up into the hundreds and it was like this joke among the family.

Over time the two cousins who were doing this made up stories of ghost, goblins and other terrifying monsters that would come around and steal the money from the eggs before they were placed and hide it in the house somewhere. It even evolved to where they were telling us that if you found it you would go insane from a spell these creatures put on it. I got to say I went along with it for a while even after I matured enough to figure out that none of it was true I went along with it was a joke against the littler cousins.

Well just this last Easter when I was collecting eggs, I noticed that there was a lot more money eggs then usual, but dismissed it as fast as I dismissed the news of my two cousins not coming this year for no specified reason.

That night I was in the dorm with my little brother when we found a loose panel in the floor. Gently lifting it, I saw a large sum of money. Gasping in disbelief, I darted for the money. Beating me to it, my little brother grabbed it, suddenly recoiling. Collapsing onto the floor, his eyes rolling into the back of his head, he started to mumble undistinguished words. Shaking him fiercely I started to panic, screaming for everyone to come help him.

Shortly after, my aunts and uncles came in with grim expressions on their faces. Slowly they came over and picked up his corpse, taking him over to the wall. My uncle James reached out slowly for a nail on the wall, pressing it further in.

To my amazement, a few of the columns of wood that made up the wall shifted up, revealing a door. Inside were two lifeless corpses. They looked like they had once been human but were now distorted with long ears and fanged teeth. Looking more closely, I saw that they were my cousins' dead bodies.

Slowly turning to me, my mom muttered under her breath, "Speak this to no one."

Five minutes later I sat there wondering what was to become of my mentality, suddenly feeling like I would go insane. Opening my mouth I tried to speak only to find that no words would come to my call. Tears rolling down my cheeks, I accepted the truth that I would never speak this to anyone. I would never speak anything to anyone ever again.

—Russell, grade11

Lesson 8:
A Completely Made-up Story

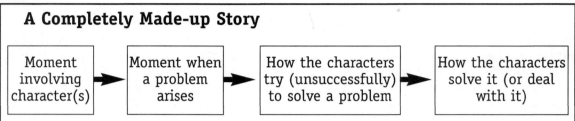

A Completely Made-up Story

| Moment involving character(s) | → | Moment when a problem arises | → | How the characters try (unsuccessfully) to solve a problem | → | How the characters solve it (or deal with it) |

Fiction sometimes does the best job of telling a story. Students sometimes like to fictionalize an experience they've had, creating characters to do the talking. They know the form. They've seen it on TV in Boy Meets World, The Wonder Years, or other series. This structure is built the same way as a memory narrative, with one difference: the content is all fictional. Students will be able to visualize the similarities between a memory piece and a fictional narrative after playing with the structure boxes.

Teaching *A Completely Made-up Story* as a Timed, Guided Writing:

(On an overhead projector, place a piece of artwork and an opinion or theme statement that correlates with a piece of literature you are reading in class, like the sample given.)

1. Look at the artwork as I read the statement to you. (*Read it aloud. Sample:* Some places have a magic all their own.)
2. Now think about a story as I read the statement again. (*Read it aloud again.*)
3. Can you imagine a story that would make an audience say this statement? In the next minute, name a character or two, and write about them for two minutes. If you can't think of anything, keep looking at the picture.
4. Take a breath and indent. For the next two minutes, tell about a problem that arises for the characters.
5. Take a breath and indent. For the next two minutes, tell how the characters try unsuccessfully to solve the problem.
6. Take a breath and indent. For the next two minutes, tell how the characters solve the problem or deal with it.

(Share either with partners or in large group, using volunteers.)

(Discuss any of the following.)
Was it easy to think of characters?
If you had more time, could you have thought of better problems and solutions?
Do you think readers would think of the original statement all on their own after having heard your story?

Teaching *A Completely Made-up Story* as a Kernel Essay:

(On an overhead projector, place a piece of artwork and an opinion or theme statement that correlates with a piece of literature you are reading in class.)

1. Read the statement with me. *(Sample:* Some places have a magic all their own.*)*
2. Think about how TV shows and movies tell their messages through stories. Can you imagine something on TV that would make audience members say this statement?

(On the blackboard or overhead, display the text structure boxes shown at the beginning of this lesson.)

3. Directly underneath the statement, copy these boxes, including the words in them.
4. Now on your paper, underneath the boxes, write one sentence to go with each of the boxes. If you'd like to draw a line from your sentence to the box, go ahead. You have about five minutes. *(Give the students writing time.)*

(Share, either with partners or in large group, using volunteers.)

Are there any moments you could expand? *(Discuss the cohesiveness or need for transitions.)*

Was this hard or easy? *(Discuss why.)*

Do you hear how each one of those kernel essays is just like a perfect plan for a whole story?

Which part should get more dialogue?

Did anyone have to add more boxes? *(Decide with the class what to do with the essays next, whether to work on them or abandon them and move on.)*

Photo by Gretchen Bernabei

138. Some places have a magic all their own.
Algunos lugares tienen su propia magia.

Truism Samples

Take the chance, even if you are scared. —Xavier

Life is nothing without fun. —Wesley

Sometimes life goes in circles. —Wesley

Life has its ups, downs, and twists. —Jacob and Sydney

Kernel Essay Samples

"I can do this," yelled Thomas a 22 year old bar tender, in a plane 25 hundred feet above the earth. Then at that second, knowing it was his turn, looking down so nervous, he saw the cars below looking like grains of sand. Then hearing a man yelling "JUMP!" he paused not knowing what to expect, then jumped! Landing, he said, "Man! that has some magic all in its own."
—Austin Green, grade 11

Full Essay Samples

Essay in the Form of a Letter
Jonathan Martinez, grade 11

Dear Diary,
　　My name is Christopher Cordena and I'm currently leading an expedition to the new world. I am the captain of my vessel and my crew, and I have been out at sea for months. I haven't a clue as to the date of this journal entry. I've decided to start this journal because of my foresight of my great popularity in the future. I also predict that this journal will be of great monetary value in later years.
　　After my crew's month at sea, we finally had landed on what I suspect to be the new world. We have also come across a strange race of people who live in little huts near rivers. These developments are peculiar and completely different from our urban cities. These people are also very dependent and in touch with the wilderness and their surroundings. I suspect that these people are like this and un-advanced because of their surroundings and the fact that they don't strive to build anything greater than their huts.
　　We Europeans, have always tried to build new things and make large amounts of money to become wealthy. I suppose I'm like this because my parents, friends and neighbors are all the same, greedy and desire many materialistic items. I have also grown up in a big and dirty city where the early wilderness was stripped away to build something more useful to people, like a shop.
　　Because of our different surroundings, the strange race of people and our viewpoints on life, society and government are very different. Although this has caused tension already, I pray it doesn't lead to confrontation.

　　　　　　　　　Sincerely,
　　　　　　　　　Christopher Cordena

Lesson 9:
A Fable

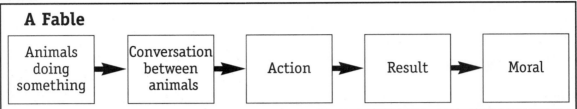

A Fable

Animals doing something → Conversation between animals → Action → Result → Moral

Sometimes people need to be warned about something, and most prompts can be revised into warnings. For instance, "It's important for people to take their time" could become the warning, "If you rush, you lose out," or "Slow and steady wins the race." This could be a useful way for students to convert a prompt into the moral at the end of a fable. It's also useful for students to recognize a fable by its organizational pattern, and not just by its moral. Then the genre becomes more truly a tool for their own use.

Teaching *A Fable* as a Timed, Guided Writing:

Do you know any fables? What fable comes to mind first? (*List ideas from students.*) What do these fables all have in common? (A story, a moral.) Think about the story before the moral. It's the story of someone who is ignoring the moral, right? Let's look at this prompt.

(*On an overhead projector, place a piece of artwork and an opinion or theme statement that correlates with a piece of literature you are reading in class, like the sample given.*)
Do people need to be warned about this?

1. Look at the artwork as I read the statement to you. (*Read it aloud. Sample: People don't know what they've got until it's gone.*) Now think about what might happen if someone didn't believe that.
2. Now, write about two animals in the middle of some activity. You have two minutes.
3. Take a breath and indent. Now, write how the first animal warns the other. You have two minutes.
4. Take a breath and indent. Now write what happens next when the second animal ignores the warning. You have two minutes.
5. Take a breath and indent. For the next two minutes, tell what happens last.

6. Take a breath and indent one more time. Now write the word "moral" and write a moral.

(Share either with partners or in large group, using volunteers.)

(Discuss any of the following.)

Did your moral work with the story?

Would you need to change anything to make the fable work better?

Did you hear anyone's fable where the whole fable made sense?

Did anyone have to make a completely new moral?

Teaching *A Fable* as a Kernel Essay:

(On an overhead projector, place a piece of artwork and an opinion or theme statement that correlates with a piece of literature you are reading in class.)

1. Read the statement with me. (*Sample:* People don't know what they've got until it's gone.)
2. See what would happen if this was written into the structure of a fable. *(On the blackboard or overhead, display the text structure boxes shown at the beginning of this lesson.)*
3. Directly underneath the statement, copy these boxes, including the words in them.
4. Now on your paper, underneath the boxes, write one sentence to go with each of the boxes. If you'd like to draw a line from your sentence to the box, go ahead. You have about five minutes. You've already got your sentence for the last box. *(Give the students writing time.)*

(Share, either with partners or in large group, using volunteers.)

Are there any parts that you could expand? *(Discuss the cohesiveness or need for transitions.)*

Was this hard or easy? *(Discuss why.)*

Do you hear how each one of those kernel essays is just like a perfect plan for a whole fable? How any one of them could be expanded into a full-blown, wonderful fable? *(Decide with the class what to do with the fables next, whether to work on them or abandon them and move on.)*

Photo courtesy of US DOD

158. Man has always created honor for the dead.
El hombre siempre ha creado honor para los muertos.

Truism Samples

Everybody eventually dies. —Jacob

Every day somebody passes away. —Sallie

You don't know what you have until it is gone. —Etan

Sometimes even though you don't think so, people really care about you. —Zach

Everyone has a time to rest. —Wesley

War means death. —Ashley

Kernel Essay Samples

Two cats are chasing a rat.
The first rat says, "Watch out, he's going to get away."
The second rat gets tired and wears himself out.
The second rat falls asleep and the rat runs away.
Moral: Don't assume everything is as it seems.

—Missy, grade 7

Full Essay Samples

Big Black Bear

There was once a big black bear that liked to bully all the other animals around, the bear would push the animals and steal from them.

"Why do you do this?" said the deer. "Why do you bully us around?"

"Because I'm a bear, and I'm bigger than you," said the bear.

All of the animals in the forest were getting tired of the bear, and his cruelty, they all hated this bear, so they all got together one night while the bear was sleeping, and thought of a plan. They decided to trap the bear in a net, and keep him there until he would be nice.

The next morning the bear woke up and found a fish lying on the ground in the middle of the forest, he looked around suspiciously, but all seemed well, so he decided to go and pick up the fish. Just as he put the fish in his mouth, and giant net came down on top of the bear. As the bear struggled the other animals came out from behind the brush and laughed at the helpless bear. The bear was rolling around and yelling at the top of his lungs, and soon rolled himself right off of a cliff. All the other animals stared horrified, they never meant for this to happen.

The next day there was a funeral for the big black bear, and all the animals came to pay their respects. Everywhere you looked there were animals crying.

"I loved that bear," said the rabbit. "I'm going to miss him."

"I loved him too," the deer cried. "He was always so nice."

Now that the bear was dead he had more friends than ever, and the animals all wished that they could tell him how much they loved him.

Moral: Treat others right today, because you never know if they will be here tomorrow.

—David Palmer, grade 12

Lesson 10:
A Sequel to a Fable

A Sequel to a Fable				
Moral of original fable	But the next day the animals said	And this happened	The result was	New moral

If you put a new twist on an old genre, you can make a new story. This structure enables students to draw on their repertoire of fables they have already heard, as a source of new creativity. Barry Lane's *The Tortoise and the Hare, Continued* models what would happen to the characters in a fable in the months and years afterward, told in fable-sized bites, each with a moral of its own. It's a wonderful model for students to imitate.

Teaching *A Sequel to a Fable* as a Timed, Guided Writing:

(Read aloud to students Barry Lane's The Tortoise and the Hare, Continued, or the student sample that follows.)

Now we're going to try one ourselves. *(On an overhead projector, place a piece of artwork and a prompt, like the sample below:* **Food can make funny memories.***)*

1. Can you think of any fables that involve food? *(Choose a short fable and read it to the class.)*
2. First, at the top of your paper, write the moral of that fable. *(For example, if you read "The Ant and the Grasshopper," the moral might be "It's good to plan ahead.")*
3. Take a breath and indent. Write "The next day…" and for the next three minutes, write what the animals said.
4. Take a breath and indent. For the next three minutes, tell what happened next.
5. Take a breath and indent. For the next three minutes, tell the outcome.
6. Take a breath and indent. Write the new moral.

(Share, either with partners or in large group, using volunteers.)

(Discuss any of the following.)

Did everyone tell the sequel the very same way?

Were the morals alike?

Where in your sequel do you think you would want to add more details?

Could you write a sequel to the sequel? What would happen the next day?

Teaching *A Sequel to a Fable* as a Kernel Essay:

(Begin by reading a fable to the class, like "The Ant and the Grasshopper.")
(On an overhead projector, place a piece of artwork and an opinion or theme statement that correlates in some way with that fable.)

1. Take a look at the sentence and the artwork, students. *(Read the statement aloud.)* Do you agree with it? If you do, copy it at the top of your page. Do you need to change some of the words to make it more true for you? If you do, go ahead and revise the sentence, and doing that will make it a prompt that you believe is true. Write your version at the top of your page.
   (On the blackboard or overhead, display the text structure boxes shown at the beginning of this lesson.)
2. Directly underneath the statement, copy these boxes, including the words in them.
3. Now on your paper, underneath the boxes, write one sentence to go with each of the boxes. If you'd like to draw a line from your sentence to the box, go ahead. You have about five minutes. You may use your statement as your new moral, in the last box. Or you may end up writing a different one. *(Give the students writing time.)*

(Share, either with partners or in large group, using volunteers.)

Did the sequel work? *(Discuss the cohesiveness or need for transitions.)*

Was it hard to write a story when you already knew the moral? *(Discuss why.)*

Do you hear how each one of those kernel essays is just like a perfect plan for a whole essay? How any one of them could be expanded into a full-blown, wonderful essay? *(Decide with the class what to do with the essays next, whether to work on them or abandon them and move on.)*

Photo by Gretchen Bernabei

007. Food can make funny memories.
La comida puede traernos memorias divertidas.

Freewriting Samples

People get into food fights and watch clowns throw pies in to other people's faces for a good laugh. Food can also be dangerous to impatient eaters who burn themselves by not letting things cool and cause funny things to happen. Then there's always the lovin' of something from the oven in American Pie. Because food is so much a part of everyone's lives, it makes for great entertainment that everyone can relate to.

—Robert Herrera, grade 9

Full Essay Samples

Once the little red hen had finished eating the bread all by herself she began to get very thirsty. She looked around for some iced tea, which was her favorite drink in the world, but there was none, so she decided that she would make some herself. She decided that she would probably need some help from the other barnyard animals to make the iced tea.

"Who will help me pick some tea leaves?" asked the hen.

"Not me," said the dog.

"Not me," said the cat.

"Not me," said the pig.

"Not me," said the turkey.

"Then I'll do it myself!" said the little red hen.

She walked over to the tree and picked a batch of tealeaves for her iced tea and put them in her basket. Then she walked back into her house to finish the job. She had enough leaves to make iced tea for everybody, so she decided to invite them all inside.

"Who will help me boil the tealeaves?" the hen asked her friends.

"Not me," said the dog.

"Not me," said the cat.

"Not me," said the pig.

"Not me," said the turkey.

"I guess I will have to do it myself then," said the exasperated hen.

So the hen walked over to the well and got a bucket of water to boil the tealeaves in. She walked back in her house and put the water on the stove and it soon began to boil. When the tealeaves were done boiling it was time to add the sugar, but the hen didn't have any sugar in her house, so she asked her friends if they wouldn't mind giving her some.

"Who will lend me a cup of sugar?" asked the hen politely.

"Not me," said the dog.

"Not me," said the cat.

"Not me," said the pig.

"Me, me," said the turkey remembering what had happened with the bread.

"Thank you, turkey," said the hen appreciatively.

So the hen and the turkey made their way to the turkey's house to get some sugar for the iced tea. When they came back all of the other barnyard animals were waiting for them in hopes of tasting the delicious iced tea. When the sugar was added and the iced tea was done, the hen and turkey both looked very satisfied at a job well done.

"Who will help us drink the tea?" asked the hen and turkey.

"Me, me," said the dog.

"Me, me," said the cat.

"Me, me," said the pig.

The hen and turkey just looked at each other and laughed, they did not want their friends to be thirsty, and so they decided to let them taste the iced tea. So for the rest of that day the five barnyard animals sat around telling stories and drinking tea. The hen and turkey were both glad that they were kind enough to share with their friends, even if they didn't get any help from them that day.

Moral: Two wrongs don't make a right.
—David Palmer, grade 12

For classroom duplication only. Enlarge at 121% for 81/2 x 11 sheet

Lesson 11:
The Story of My Thinking

The Story of My Thinking

| What I used to think | but this happened | so now I think |

Because we are human, we grow. We have experiences that change what we think, or deepen what we think, or add nuances to what we think. So thoughts we had months or years ago will continue to change in depth or substance as our years add layers to our lives.

For instance, as an American citizen, I grew up thinking that our nation was pretty safe and secure. But then America experienced the tragedy of September 11. Now I'm aware, along with the whole nation, that our country isn't as impenetrable as I had thought; that we're vulnerable.

So when students find a "truism" in a prompt, they can stop and think about how that truth has developed in their eyes, through their experience. And whatever truth is in the prompt, the students' understanding of it has changed.

This text structure creates an essay that traces the movement of the student's mind and tells the story of the thought. It converts analysis into a narrative form, making it easier for a reader to follow. The ending definitely doesn't restate the beginning; rather, the thought moves from "then" to "now."

Teaching *The Story of My Thinking* as a Timed, Guided Writing:

(Give students three index cards. Have them number the cards.)

First, I'm going to show you how this works, with a demonstration.
Everybody's thinking changes, depending on what they go through. Ideas change. Here's an example of my own thinking, and how it's changed:

I used to think that teachers who didn't have children could be just as understanding as teachers who do have children. Then I had a daughter. I realized when Matilde started school that parents don't just want their children to be treated fairly, or to learn valuable lessons. I felt sheer terror for her that she'd go through pain and I wouldn't be there to help her, to protect her. Real terror, the kind you can't talk about without getting tears. I realized my mother felt it when I went to school, an unspeakable ache. So when parents now ask me if I have children, I look into their eyes and know. It's shared terror.

So, I used to think that teachers don't have to be parents in order to be effective with children. Then I had Matilde. Now I understand what parents worry about when their children go to school, and other parents are the only other people who completely understand it.
Now we're going to try one together.

(On an overhead projector, place a piece of artwork and an opinion or theme statement that correlates with a piece of literature you are reading in class. Sample: Life is so fragile.)
Look at the statement. Do you believe it's true? Copy it down on card #3. (If you don't believe it's true, then change it to make it true, a statement you believe.)

Now, think about it. Did you always know it was true? How has your thinking about it changed? Some things have happened in your life that have given you a different understanding of that sentence from the one you had some years ago.

Think of one thing that happened in your life that taught you how true the statement is. This is going on the #2 card. For the next three minutes, write down one event in your life, small or large, that showed you that this statement is true. Write in as much detail as you can fit onto the card in three minutes.

Now, that leaves the #1 card. Any speculations about what's going on there? *(Listen, maybe taking note of some ideas to try later.)* Look at the #3 card. That's what you believe is true now, but in your old days, you didn't understand it the same way. Think back a few years, and write what you used to think. Write it on the #1 card.

(Share, either with partners or in large group, using volunteers.)
(Discuss any of the following.)
Do you think people keep any of their thoughts exactly the same?
Was it difficult to word the #1 card, to show slight changes?
Did the #1 card reflect a different kind of "knowing" from the #3 card?
Can you see that depending on the prompt, you might use it either as the #1 or the #3 card?

Teaching *The Story of My Thinking* as a Kernel Essay:

(On an overhead projector, place a piece of artwork and an opinion or theme statement that correlates with a piece of literature you are reading in class. Sample: Life is so fragile.*)*

1. Take a look at the sentence and the artwork, students. *(Read the statement aloud.)* Do you agree with it? If you do, copy it at the top of your page. Do you need to change some of the words to make it more true for you? If you do, go ahead and revise the sentence, and doing that will make it a prompt that you believe is true. Write your version at the top of your page.
   (On the blackboard or overhead, display the text structure boxes shown at the beginning of this lesson.)
2. Directly underneath the statement, copy these boxes, including the words in them.
3. Now on your paper, underneath the boxes, write one sentence to go with each of the boxes. If you'd like to draw a line from your sentence to the box, go ahead. You have about five minutes. You've already got your sentence for one of the boxes. *(Give the students writing time.)*

(Share, either with partners or in large group, using volunteers.)

Did the kernel essays ring true?

Do you hear how powerful these thoughts are?

Is this a useful text structure that you could imagine using when you write "to a prompt"?

Do you hear how each one of those kernel essays is just like a perfect plan for a whole essay?

Which part would you most likely expand to make this a full-blown, wonderful essay? *(Decide with the class what to do with the essays next, whether to work on them or abandon them and move on.)*

Photo courtesy of USDA

244. Life is so fragile.
La vida es tan frágil.

Truism Samples

Sometimes you need help to reach your goals. —Sydney

Life is a journey. —Xavier

Everyone has their obstacle. —Sallie

Guided Writing Samples

I used to think that I didn't need people (a.k.a. my parents) worrying about me when I was out with my friends at night, because I thought I would never get myself in trouble.

Then one night I ran into some problems, so I came home early to have my parents help me deal with it...but they were out because they weren't expecting until later.

Now I think that it is comforting to know my parents are at home wondering where I am and ready to offer help whenever I'm in trouble.

—Heather Brunts, grade 11

Kernel Essay Samples

I used to think the candy man would eat me. But I dreamed about him eating me. Now I think I'm stronger than him.

—Kendrick, grade 4

I used to believe in Santa. But I was up all night and peeking out other door. I got in trouble. Now I think, we'll pretend that he is real because of the little kids.

—Amanda, grade 4

I used to think that drama wasn't really part of my life. Nothing exciting or bad ever really happened. Then, I became a teenager and went to high school. Now I think that drama is an everyday thing!

—Jennifer Johnson, grade 11

I used to think that my father never cared about my dancing and about my competitions. Then, during our dance performance, I saw him walk in. Now I know he believes in me and supports me in everything I do.

—Samantha Cortes, grade 11

Full Essay Samples

Take It or Leave It

Standing on the end of the three-meter diving board, my leg muscles trembled with nervousness. I saw my coaches' serious faces looking up at me from down below telling me I was ready. I heard all my teammates cheering me on while they waited for my attempt at an inward two-and-a-half. My mind began racing as I thought to myself: Will I make it? Will I be close to the board? I really want to do this! You can do this!

I dive at the Josh Davis Natatorium at Blossom Athletic Center on the San Antonio Divers National Team. It is a beautiful pool consisting of two sets of one-meters and two three-meters. We also enjoy the luxury of three extremely bouncing trampolines, as well as a very well equipped weight room in which we use frequently. I am at my pool a very large portion of my life. I love the atmosphere there. It is my home away from home.

It all started when I walked through the two sets of double doors on the bring pool deck. As soon as I walked in, I could smell the strong scent of chlorine. I place my bag on the floor next to a brick wall and then carefully head over to the back of the deck because the floor is as slippery as an ice rink. Once I arrive I sit down on one of the mats neatly set out for our exercises. I started chattering with one of my good friends named Kali. "So I heard today is a new dive day," droned Kali.

"Yeah me too. I'm sort of nervous!" I replied.

"I think I have to do a+ back one-and-a-half tuck over three-meter," croaked Kali.

"Really, I'm not sure what I have to do yet."

Usually I jump on the trampoline before practice starts, but since Allison or Craig (my coaches) weren't around, Kali and I just kept on chatting while other people started showing up. I love how our team is so close and we get along so well, but right at 4:30 it's time to get serious. Allison and Craig come out of their office and begin telling us exercises to start to get us warmed up before heading to the boards. A major goal for my coaches is to get us into shape so we do a ton of dry-land which includes: abs, flipping on the pits, jumping on the trampolines, weight room, modeling our dives, and tumbling.

After a tough work out all of our sweaty bodies start to head over to the boards. I stop to get a cool, refreshing drink from the water fountain and then continue walking until I reach my bag. I strap on my suit and drift over to the whiteboard with everyone else. Here our coaches explain our workout. "Today is New Dive Day!" Craig boomed with an excited look on his face.

"Yes and I know you all are scared, but I want you to try you new dives anyway," explains Allison.

"Here is a list of everyone's name and their appropriate new dive," instructed Craig.

"Start with some lead-ups, then let's go!" cries Allison.

I glace up at the board and find my name. I slowly move my eyes to the right and see 405C, inward two-and-a-half off three-meter. All the sudden I feel a big surge of adrenalin rush through my body. I really wanted to do this dive but I was scared.

Standing on the end of the three-meter diving board, my leg muscles trembling with nervousness. I could feel my coach's serious face looking up at me. I heard all my teammates cheering me on while they waited for my attempt at an inward-two-and-a-half. My mind raced as I thought to myself: Will I make it? Will I be close to the board? I really wanted to do this! Can you do this! I knew in my mind I had to turn my brain off and just throw the dive. I literally felt like I couldn't feel my legs anymore. Finally I decided once and for all to just count to three and go.

"1 ... 2 ... 3 ... GO!" I cried to myself, but after "GO!" I was still impatiently shivering on the end of the board.

Once again I slowly counted to three.

"1 ... 2 ... 3 ... GO!"

I started my back press, but unexpectedly lose my balance and almost fall off the board. By now I begin to grow extremely impatient and losing important confidence. It is frustrating to have to wait to do something that is frightening to you and out of your comfort zone. Finally I say to myself, this is it or you're getting off the board. Once again I whisper confidently to myself

"1 ... 2 ... 3 ... GO!"

I begin my back press with negatives thoughts racing through my brain. I block them out immediately as I push off the board and throw my straight in front of me as fast as I could. Before I knew it I'm spinning through the air like an acrobat and after completing two-and-a-half summersaults, land in the water. I lift my head out of the water and hear roars of applause and cheering from my coaches and teammates. It felt really good to get out of the water knowing I just successfully attempted an inward two-and-a-half off three-meter. There aren't many better feelings than that.

I used to think I was too much of a "caution-freak" and didn't take any risks. Then this happened. Now I think that every diving practice I go to is a major risk and I'm always trying new, exciting things. Sometimes you have to take risks. It's part of life.

—Samantha Holland, grade 7

For classroom duplication only. Enlarge at 121% for 81/2 x 11 sheet

56   **Reviving The Essay** © 2005 Discover Writing Press • www.discoverwriting.com

Is The Truth the Best Policy?

From the time I was old enough to speak, I had strict parents that would turn my butt black and blue for the slightest thing I did wrong. I would always feel compelled to save my butt from an interesting shade of purple. I would lie and deceive my parents to get out of trouble. Sometimes it would work and sometimes I would have to walk into my room and see my dad with his belt in his hand, and I would think to myself, was it worth it? Well eventually I grew out of spankings and I would get a punishment way worse than the crime. I learned if you tell them your version of the truth, nobody suffers any heartache. That theory was put to rest a few months ago.

I had just gotten my driver's license and was going out every night. Well, one night I told my parents that I was going to Helotes to be with my girl. My girl lived over by Madison High School, which in my parent's eye might and well be on the other side of the world. All night we just sat around and basically did what I told my parents I would be doing. When I left, something happened that could only happen to me.

As I was backing out, I hit my girl's mother's car. My girl's mom was standing right there. No real damage had been done, just a scratch. So, we left the insurance companies out of it, however a police report was filled out. Now I was faced with a decision. Do I tell the folks or hope to god it goes away. It was a long ride home. As I drove the truck, I watched the white lines in the payment pass by and I thought to myself about how many parties and how many privileges I would be loosing. I preyed that dad wasn't awake because I knew it would be easier to tell him. At least it would be easier than telling my mother.

As I pulled into the driveway, I parked the truck and sat inside telling myself, "you have to tell them, it's better if they find out from you than them." I kept repeating this to myself over and over. I finally walked into the house and into the bed room and saw a cold chilling sight. My dad was sound asleep and my mom was awake. The feeling I got when I hit the car came back to me again. I got my mom into the kitchen and just hit her between the eyes with the truth. All except where I was. Then she asked…"where were you again?" I had to tell her and I did. She wasn't happy about where I was, but to my surprise she didn't kill me. She told me that I acted like an adult and since things were taken care of, to not let it happen again. I went to bed feeling relieved.

This incident showed me that sometimes it's just better to be straight with people. If I had lied, I would have been a nervous wreck all week. But knowing that it was out in the open and everything was okay, I had nothing to worry about. Now, me and my parents are real straight with each other. I learned a valuable lesson. When you are too deep and it's way over your head, truth is just the best policy.

—Kyle Lockamy, grade 11

Lesson 12:
Comparing Notes (Mine and Others')

Comparing Notes (Mine and Others')

| Some people think | and | other people think | but | I think | what could change my thinking |

Sometimes it's worthwhile to mull over differing points of view. In this text structure, students are guided to gather up differing points of view that they have noticed, and to explain them.

Teaching *Comparing Notes* as a Timed, Guided Writing:

(Give students four index cards. Have them number the cards.)

(On an overhead projector, place a piece of artwork and an opinion or theme statement that correlates with a piece of literature you are reading in class. Sample: Children and grown-ups see things in different ways.*)*

1. Look at the artwork.
2. Do you believe that statement is true? If you do, copy it. If you need to change it to make it true for you, go ahead.
3. For the next minute, on the same card, explain the statement. (What does it mean? What is your interpretation of it?) *(Give the students two minutes.)* Now, put that card aside.
4. Can you imagine someone who might disagree with your statement? What version of the statement would they say is true? (*Example:* Children and grown-ups see certain things the same way.) Go ahead and write down the new version, or use my example if you can't think of one. Now, for the next two minutes and on the same card, explain how some people might think that statement is true.
5. Can you think of any other version that other people might think is true? (*Example:* Some people think that teenagers see things the way both children and adults see them. *Or:* Some people think that children and grown-ups see love the same way, but everything else they see differently.) Write down this version on the next card, and explain it in the next two minutes. *(Give the students writing time.)* Now, put that card aside.

Reviving The Essay © 2005 Discover Writing Press • www.discoverwriting.com

6. Last, consider why people think about this idea in different ways. How do you explain the differences? Most important, what would have to happen to change your own thinking about this? On the last card, write "what might change my thinking?" And spend the next two minutes answering that.

7. Now you have four cards. Put them into whatever order you think would be interesting or effective.

(Share, either with partners or in large group, using volunteers.)

(Discuss any of the following.)

Would these make good essays?

How different were the thoughts?

How easy would it be to find evidence for each of the cards?

Is there any one card that didn't fit? Would your piece of writing be better without one of the cards?

Teaching *Comparing Notes* as a Kernel Essay:

(On an overhead projector, place a piece of artwork and an opinion or theme statement that correlates with a piece of literature you are reading in class. Sample: Children and grown-ups see things in different ways.*)*

1. Take a look at the sentence and the artwork, students. *(Read the statement aloud.)* Do you agree with it? If you do, copy it at the top of your page. Do you need to change some of the words to make it more true for you? If you do, go ahead and revise the sentence, and doing that will make it a prompt that you believe is true. Write your version at the top of your page.
   (On the blackboard or overhead, display the text structure boxes shown at the beginning of this lesson.)

2. Directly underneath the statement, copy these boxes, including the words in them.

3. Now on your paper, underneath the boxes, write one sentence to go with each of the boxes. If you'd like to draw a line from your sentence to the box, go ahead. You have about five minutes. You've already got your sentence for one of the boxes. You just have to decide which box it goes into. *(Give the students writing time.)*

(Share, either with partners or in large group, using volunteers.)

Do the sentences work together smoothly? *(Discuss the cohesiveness or need for transitions.)*

Was this hard or easy? *(Discuss why.)*

Do you hear how each one of those kernel essays is just like a perfect plan for a whole essay? Into which of these parts would you add some examples or illustrations, and expand this essay?

Where would you get the examples for these parts? (Literature? History? Personal experience?) *(Decide with the class what to do with the essays next, whether to work on them or abandon them and move on.)*

Photo courtesy of the Dee Nall Family

046. Children and grown-ups see things in different ways.
Los niños y los adultos ven las cosas de diferente manera.

Truism Samples

Everyone can reach different heights. —Lindsey

Sometimes you need help to get to the top. —Kiylei

Do what you want to do. —Kaijah

Always reach for the stars. —Traevon

You can always get to the top. —Gardi

Freewriting Samples

Children and grown-ups do think differently. I should know because my mom and I most all the time think differently. The reason I say that is because the first time I wanted to spend the night at a friend's house, my mom and dad had some doubts, because they didn't know her parents. I thought, why not? Then later I saw how they thought. I never knew how much differently our minds thought.
—Elysia Alvarez, grade 9

I think grown-ups and kids see things differently. What kids see as fun, grown-ups see as dangerous. Like if a kid wanted to go into the woods because he/she thinks it might be fun: the parent would think that it's dangerous because a kid can get kidnapped. I used to think hanging out in the woods was cool, but I now know what can happen.

 —Aaron Perez, grade 9

Kernel Essay Samples

Some people think that aging will be horrible and try to avoid it.
Other people think that aging is wonderful and will love it.
I personally don't want to age, and am not looking forward to being old.
I guess that if I grow up to be a happy old lady, then I'll know I was wrong.

 —Mari Compean, grade 11

Full Essay Samples

War is a part of our world, simple as that.

 I had been talking to my dad about war in general but more specifically it came down to me, him and my cousin debating if we had just cause to "liberate" Iraq. My dad kept bringing up how the people were being killed by Saddam Hussein and how Iraq had all these weapons of mass destructions etc. Just so you know my dad is a right wing republican that eats anything the news/president throws at him.

 My cousin, not quite as blind, argued that we should have waited longer to attack Iraq and had a better cause than liberating people who had never asked to be liberated and to expunge all of the weapons of mass destruction Saddam had.

 Needless to say I agreed more with my cousin. Even though we had probable cause to attack Saddam, I personally do not think violence solves conflict. To this day no weapons of mass destruction have been found, almost every day I hear of troops being killed by suicide bombers that are Iraqis, and that we still have not found Saddam Hussein. In the future this time may be reflected on as a "one step backwards for two steps forward" but right now I think U.S. citizens are waging a war that could have been resolved in a better fashion.

 If we (the United States) had evidence that proved one-hundred percent that Saddam had weapons of mass destruction and was an immediate, and I mean absolutely immediate threat to national security (before we had provoked them to do anything that would be considered as endangering national security) then we would have a reason to attack Iraq. Only at that point would I support any aggression towards Iraq. The damage is done; let's just hope in the future we don't shoot ourselves in the foot again.

 —Russell, grade 11

Lesson 13:
Evolution of a Term

Evolution of a Term

What the word meant to me when I was 4	What the word meant to me when I was 10	What the word means to me now	What the word will probably mean when I am _____ (pick an age)

Vygotsky teaches us the amazing history of the development of thought and language, visible in the way the meaning of one word changes as we grow. This exercise accomplishes the layering of richness of meaning, as we live through experiences. This structure also gives a narrative structure to an abstract idea.

Teaching *Evolution of a Term* as a Timed, Guided Writing:

(On an overhead projector, place a piece of artwork and an opinion or theme statement that correlates with a piece of literature you are reading in class. Sample: It's easy to be deceived by a person's appearance.*)*

1. Look at the prompt. Choose the most important word or phrase, the part that means the most to you. Write that word or phrase in the margin.
2. Now for the next three minutes, write what that word or phrase meant to you when you were little, say when you were four or five years old.
3. Take a breath, indent, and look at the word or phrase you selected again. What did that word or phrase mean to you when you were ten? Tell that for the next three minutes.
4. Take a breath, indent, and look at the word or phrase you selected again. What does it mean to you now? Tell that for the next three minutes.
5. Take a breath, indent, and look one more time at the word or phrase you began with. What do you think it will mean to you in the future? Tell that for the next couple of minutes.

(Share, either with partners or in large group, using volunteers.)
(Discuss any of the following.)
Did the meaning of the word or phrase change much? Why?
How many writers began their paragraphs with "when I was four" or "when I was ten"? How could we change those so that the essays are not all the same?

Teaching *Evolution of a Term* as a Kernel Essay:

(On an overhead projector, place a piece of artwork and an opinion or theme statement that correlates with a piece of literature you are reading in class. Sample: It's easy to be deceived by a person's appearance.*)*

1. Take a look at the sentence and the artwork, students. (Read the statement aloud.)
2. What word or phrase in the prompt do you consider most important, or most interesting? Write that word or phrase at the top of your page.
   (On the blackboard or overhead, display the text structure boxes shown at the beginning of this lesson.)
3. Directly underneath the statement, copy these boxes, including the words in them.
4. Now on your paper, underneath the boxes, write one sentence to go with each of the boxes. If you'd like to draw a line from your sentence to the box, go ahead. You have about five minutes. *(Give the students writing time.)*
   (Share, either with partners or in large group, using volunteers.)
Do the sentences all "hang together"? *(Discuss the cohesiveness or need for transitions.)*
Was this hard or easy? *(Discuss why.)*
Do you hear how each one of those kernel essays is just like a perfect plan for a whole essay?
Which section would be most interesting to explain? *(Decide with the class what to do with the essays next, whether to work on them or abandon them and move on.)*

Spin-offs:

This exercise works well as a gift or thank-you note, when the word or phrase has to do with a person.

Give every student a few minutes with a list of quotations and let each student choose a quotation they believe is true. The resulting drafts are different and fascinating.

Revision idea: After at least three students read their drafts aloud, the sameness of paragraph openings appears as a problem, making the papers seem formulaic. Experiment with ways to "hide the seams" and create more personalized links from paragraph to paragraph.

Photo by Gretchen Bernabei

039. Sometimes a simple thing can change your whole image.
Algunas veces un detalle pequeño puede cambiar nuestra imagen completa.

Truism Samples

It's easy to be deceived by someone's appearance. —Margo

People aren't always what they seem to be. —Matthew

We all wear masks of different kinds. —John

Guided Writing Samples

The Big Word

The word DECEIVE is something that I didn't understand when I was four years old. It was something that I was not prepared to deal with. How was I going to know what was happening? You don't believe in lies at that age. Every time that somebody says "I promise" or "he told me" or things that you can not fight with.

I know this because there is nothing better than my own experience. It all began when my parents were getting a divorce. Since then I started to understand the word and why the people do it, and I found out that my parents did it to me. Maybe they did because they didn't want to lose me or maybe because they didn't like each other. Many problems arose during that time and there were many things each told me about the other (bad stuff) that I believed, but I later found out that they were both wrong.

Now I'm seventeen years old and even though I grew up, the people keep deceiving me. It is incredible how many ways there are to tell a lie. They might not do it in an "evil" way, but sometimes they do. We can see it all the time, we just have to turn on the TV and see the "ultra, mega, super produce" they're selling.

Also every time that I work on the street and I see the posters saying good things about their products. I stop and think, why is your product the best and dose it have something that nobody else has in the street next to their poster saying the same thing about their "Super Product?"

DECEIVE, it is a big word. Many people take advantage of this and I'm sure that I will have many experiences with this when I grown up. Maybe when I'm forty five years old, it might have some meaning, but I strongly think that this all depends on my social, economic, and cultural status. When I say this, I mean that people will take advantage of what you have or know.

—Arturo Soler, grade 11

Kernel Essay Samples

When I was young, I used to think glasses would make me cool. Now I think glasses won't make me look cool, but maybe if they were nice glasses they would make me look better. When I'm 45 I probably won't care whether glasses make my not-so-good-looking face look better.

—Gabriel Lopez, grade 9

I used to think that image wasn't important until I hit middle school. I remember that some preppy girl wore Converse to school. Automatically she looked like a poser. Now I stay in my own "league" and never change into something I'm not.

—Stephanie Lagrow, grade 9

Full Essay Samples

When I was four, the word "daddy" meant hugs and laughter. It meant a giant of a man with strong hands and shoulders that were good for riding. Daddy meant stories before bedtime when the soft light and soft voices lulled me into safe dreams with "Good Night Moon" chanting in my ears. Daddy was safety and warmth, certainty and love.

But when I was 10, the word "daddy" changed. No longer did I associate the word with the warmth and safety of childhood. Daddy became someone who went away and didn't come back. Daddy was someone who not only left my mom, but he left me as well. At first, he would call and visit, but then he moved away. He married Trisha, and the phone calls became less and less. There was always a reason why he couldn't or didn't visit. It was hard for me to remember those safe nights and strong arms.

Now "daddy" is something I miss, I long for. I look at my friends who fight with their dads or get mad when they can't go somewhere and do something because their dads just don't understand. I feel jealous. I wish my dad was around to tell me I could or couldn't do something. Sometimes I associate the word "daddy" with anger and resentment. But mostly, I just associate it with missing someone really badly.

I hope that when I am 21 or 22, I won't feel so sad or mad when I think of "daddy." Who knows? Maybe my dad will come back into my life. I wonder who will walk me down the aisle when I get married. I wonder if my own kids will miss having a "grandpa" the way I have missed having a daddy.

So many questions....I keep remembering "Good night, Moon."

—Sarah, grade 8
Student of Cathy D'Entrement

Reviving The Essay © 2005 Discover Writing Press • www.discoverwriting.com

The Phrases We Love to Hear

Trust. A word we all seem to find security in. Friendships, families, jobs and relationships all rely on it. I promise you. You can always believe me. I'll never hurt you. All phrases we love to hear. Why? How could you? You told me you wouldn't. When the balm to our ears becomes the tears in our eyes, we begin to question others' faithfulness to us.

I remember walking into my kindergarten class and feeling overwhelmed with anxiety of all types. None of the wondering faces looked familiar to me. I saw little girls crying for their mothers, little boys already beginning to explore and bond, and then a little read headed girl sitting at a table alone. "Maybe I should go sit with her?" Megan and I became friends instantly. We brightened Mrs. Rigby's days with our constant whispers and giggles. She was my first real friend and for that school year we were connected at the hip. We promised each other that we would always be best friends. The pact the two of us made meant the world to me and my naive heart.

During the summer after kindergarten, her family moved away and I never heard from Megan again. Although today I couldn't tell you her last name, and doubt I even knew then, when Megan told me we'd be friends forever, I believed her. Her moving made me realize that promises friends make aren't always forever. Had it been that they were intentionally or unintentionally broken or not. Although I was a fairly young girl, I learned many things that year about trust and pain.

After that, for a long time I thought that the only people I would ever truly trust was my family. Of course I had friends afterwards, but always in the back of my mind there was that unanswered doubt about everything they told me. Then I met Roy. I remember walking into my eighth grade reading class and, after about half the year, seeing him. He looked mysterious, and that interested me. I thought, "he looks like a very interesting guy." We became friends and were for about a year, and then we ended up getting together. For that year I was so happy and finally began to trust again.

A lot of things happened that ended our relationship, and when I look at it from the outside I realize that so much of what he had told me were lies. Sometimes we are just too wrapped up in the good things to realize it. I felt like a fool, and because of him, once again trusting people was a very hard thing for me to do. He told me he would never hurt me and he did.

Even though it's been years since kindergarten and almost one since the end of me and Roy, those are two examples of trust broken in my life that affect me a lot. Still to this day, I have a lot of issues with trusting people. I've realized that everyone lies, and that a promise is only false hope put into words, that are rarely kept true. Once trust is broken, it can never truly be revived. Every instance of unfaithfulness that we experience is forever in betted in our minds and hearts and slowly makes us wonder if should really believe those phrases we love to hear.

—Kelsey Hall, grade 11

Lesson 14:
Tribute to the Person Who Taught Me Something

Tribute to the Person Who Taught Me Something				
What the lesson is	Flashback to the lesson	Description of the person	Lyrics or words you can remember that person saying (on any subject)	What I wish I could find out now from that person

Most of what we really know has come to us through another person. If Wilbur the pig knows loyalty, it's because of his friend Charlotte. If Scout Finch knows fairness, it's because of her father Atticus. Because we connect so strongly to other people, it's sometimes easier to consider who taught us something than to focus on our abstract ideas and beliefs. Those people don't have to be fictional characters, though. The students who lost Lara Wiedenfeld, their fourth-grade teacher, would say that she taught them lessons about life and love.

This text structure emphasizes a person. It turns a prompt into a lesson taught to us by one of our mentors. It also provides a valuable starting point for experimenting with personally meaningful "thick description," which will be covered thoroughly in Chapter 3.

Teaching *Tribute to a Person* as a Timed, Guided Writing:

(Give students five index cards or slips of paper. On an overhead projector, place a piece of artwork and an opinion or theme statement that correlates with a piece of literature you are reading in class, like the sample: Every family has its heroes.)

1. Look at the artwork. Next, read the statement with me. Do you believe it's true? Is it one of life's lessons that you've learned? If it is, copy it onto the first index card. For the next two minutes, explain what that statement means. If you need to change the statement, so that it will be truly one of the lessons you've learned in your life, go ahead and change it. Then explain what the statement means.
2. Think about who in your life most helped you know that statement is true, or who helped you learn that lesson. On the next card, name the person and describe him or her. (Give them a few minutes.)
3. Think back to one moment when you learned the lesson. On the next card, tell the story of that moment. This card will be like a flashback to that moment. (Give them a few minutes.)
4. Think about the person again, and about how well you know them. Think about some things you can imagine hearing them say, often. Or imagine that person

singing. When they come through the door, or just at any time, what do you imagine them saying or singing? Write down some phrases you remember them saying or singing on the next card. (Give them a few minutes.)

5. Now, on the last card, write down one thing you wish that person could teach you now. (Give them a few minutes.)

6. Now you have five pieces of your relationship on that card. Put the cards in what ever order you think would make the best piece of writing.

(Share, either with partners or in large group, using volunteers.)

(Discuss any of the following.)

How did you arrange your cards? (Compare and celebrate variations.)

Did you notice your mood changing as you wrote the cards? How? Why? (Discuss the nature of a tribute.)

In turning these cards into an essay, what would you need to add? (Talk through ways to develop parts.)

What would you do with the "words they say" card? How could you use those through your paper?

What part made you feel most connected to the person you were writing about?

Teaching *Tribute to a Person* as a Kernel Essay:

(On an overhead projector, place a piece of artwork and an opinion or theme statement that correlates with a piece of literature you are reading in class.)

1. Take a look at the sentence and the artwork, students. *(Read the statement aloud. Sample:* Every family has its heroes.) Do you agree with it? If you do, copy it at the top of your page. Do you need to change some of the words to make it more true for you? If you do, go ahead and revise the sentence, and doing that will make it a prompt that you believe is true. Write your version at the top of your page. *(On the blackboard or overhead, display the text structure boxes shown at the beginning of this lesson.)*

2. Directly underneath the statement, copy these boxes, including the words in them.

3. Now on your paper, underneath the boxes, write one sentence to go with each of the boxes. If you'd like to draw a line from your sentence to the box, go ahead. You have about five minutes. You've already got your sentence for the first box. *(Give the students writing time.)*

(Share, either with partners or in large group, using volunteers.)

(Discuss any of the following.)

Do the sentences all "hang together"? *(Discuss the cohesiveness or need for transitions.)*

Was this hard or easy? *(Discuss why.)*

Do you hear how each one of those kernel essays is just like a perfect plan for a whole essay? How any one of them could be expanded into a full-blown, wonderful essay? *(Decide with the class what to do with the essays next, whether to work on them or abandon them and move on. These essays make wonderful gifts for the person featured, and they make powerful classroom anthologies if you collect them and bind them together.)*

Guided Writing Samples

Dear Mom,

Over the years the time we shared was unimaginable. The long walks and evening talks which sometimes lasted into the morning. It seemed like never ending laughter in our home. Even the time I lost your favorite pair of earrings. You still didn't stop loving me. The cooking lessons you put me through to prepare me for college life. How hard you worked to ensure me money for college. All my extra-curricular activities from volleyball games, to spelling bees you attended. You were there for me when my first love broke my heart. Every Sunday you made sure we went to Church. You instilled discipline and good work ethics in me. You made sure when I got my license to warn everyone but you still let me drive the car even after I hit the trashcan. You always told me everything would be ok. You prepared me to live on my own and taught me how to clean the toilet. You made sure I was taken care of because you knew one day I would be on my own. What you taught me I still apply to my life everyday. I didn't expect you to leave so soon and knew I understand why you taught me everything at a young age. Every Sunday I go to Church. It helps me get a little closer to you. You were the person who impacted my life the most in everything I do. Even the simple things make me think of you. I take a walk every evening and think of all the things you taught me. I remember the time you had to buy new trashcans because you let me use the car. You made an impact in my heart like the impact a rock has on the moon. It was you who made me understand life.

> With all my love,
> Your daughter Jennifer

—Jenny M Cook, grade 10

Photo of Charles Sharp by Adam Sharp. Courtesy of Meghan Sharp

162. Every family has its heroes.
Cada familia tiene sus héroes.

Truism Samples

Everyone is remembered by someone. —Wesley

Everyone gets tired. —Jessica

Pictures can hold memories for life. —Kaijah

Everyone has to close their eyes sometime. —Toni

Growing old isn't a scary thing. —Kiylei

Guided Writing Samples

Some things are worth working for. I need to do that because I want a Playstation 2 and mom says that I have to earn the money myself. That's what starts my big adventure.

I was walking to my first house to mow and earn $20 if I did both front and back. I went to the house and finished both sides in 10 min. Then the lady said if I vacuumed upstairs I would earn $10. After that I walked 15 dogs at once (they all liked each other because they all were golden retrievers). I earned $5 from each of the owners (each owner had 1). Now I have a question. It goes like this: 20+10=30 and 15x5=75, so I'm almost there.

My mom taught me this lesson. She had said "Earn your money yourself or get it when you get older."

Now I want to know how I can earn money easier than what I did.

—Parth, grade 4
Student of Lara Wiedenfeld

Some things are worth working for. I try hard to be a good sister. Some roads are smooth others are rocky. But so far I'm doing pretty good. When they annoy me sometimes I just feel like socking them. But somehow I don't. Being a good sister is hard, but it's worth it.

I haven't yet reached my goal, but my two sisters push me. Sometimes I want to quit. But remembering them I feel I must go on. My goal is harder than it seems. Doing the right thing. Facing the facts. It's hard, but I will do almost anything for my sisters.

I can't believe they showed me how to be kind to them. When they struck age 2 my life changed forever. I had to accept them pulling my hair, messing up my stuff. I had to be nice to them. Now I don't want to learn any more from my younger sisters.

—Bailey, grade 4
Student of Lara Wiedenfeld

Kernel Essay Samples

Alec taught me friendship is a good thing. He taught me by becoming my friend and making him and I happy. Alec was playful, fun, smart, nice, and creative. "Let's watch TV!" If I could talk to him now, I could find out what life is like in Wisconsin.

—Kevin, grade 4

I stole money from people at HEB. I learned my lesson is that I never steal money. And I never will do that. My cousin told me to never do that or it's time for a whoopen. My cousin Gardi is 11 years old. His b-day is June 13, 1994. His favorite song is Usher. He hugs me every day. He sometimes says, "I love you Doris." I wish he would teach me to never talk back to your parents.

—Doris, grade 4

The Difference in My Life

My mom Gianet Brown is a strong woman. She cleans, cooks, washes clothes, helps me with my schoolwork and most of all, she shows me love and support. She inspired me to be somebody in life, and she made a difference in my life, and I know now she is a true queen.

My mom used to be sick. And she told me all the time, if she dies, I have to clean, cook and wash clothes for myself. But I didn't think she was that sick. She taught me how to cook and do other things as I developed into a young lady. But one day when she showed me a tape about children who lost their parents, it made me think hard. And as I watched, I started to cry as if it were my own mom. I told her that I was sorry for talking back, all the attitudes, and for disrespecting and disobeying her. The next morning when I arrived at school, they told me my mom was taken into the hospital for an operation.

I screamed, panicked and cried as if my mother were already dead. I felt like the children on that tape, and now I know what she meant to tell me all these years of my life, that one day she will die and I will have to go on with my life to become someone.

After school, my aunt took me to go see her. She was asleep. But when I looked at her I had that feeling again, like she was dead already. When she woke up, I couldn't hug her cause she was in pain, but when I kissed her it was the flood of tears.

After this experience, it made me realize how it is for children to lose their parents. It was hard seeing my mom in the hospital, and when we talked it was like we were at home. "Mom. How are you feeling today?" "I'm okay. Don't worry." "Are you sure? Do you need anything from the store?" "Yes, sweetie, I'm fine." "Well today at school was okay." "Well today at the hospital was boring." My mom likes to joke around a lot. But I know when she is solemn, and know when I look into her eyes, it can probably be the last time. My point is my mom made me realize if she were gone what I would do. And since that experience, I've tried hard to treat her like a queen, because I never know when she can disappear like a zephyr.

—Varecia Brown, grade 7

For classroom duplication only. Enlarge at 121% for 81/2 x 11 sheet

Reviving The Essay © 2005 Discover Writing Press • www.discoverwriting.com   73

Nothing Is As Fascinating As Playing With Danger

Well my friend "Junior" Marco he's about 5'9", or 5' 10". He's built, but chunky. He has dark brown hair, and dark brown eyes. His skin is Carmel colored. He wear's glasses. He's very funny, and has a wonderful sense of humor. He smiles a lot, and he's very down to earth. He loves to go to parties, and to the mall to chill hang out with me, my brother Moses "Moe" and his cousin Emanuel "Manny." Junior still goes to school at "S.A.C" San Antonio College.

Well, two weeks ago, on Saturday, we were supposed to go to the movies all four of us, Moses, Marco "Jr.", Emanuel "Manny" and myself. We stopped for about ten to twelve minutes to chill out and get some money for Manny. Well Jr. showed me a gun that was empty at the moment. I saw the barrel empty. He aimed the gun towards me and I told him, "Put he gun away!" He showed me two kinds of bullets. One was hollowed out and the other was not hollowed. I asked him, "What's the difference between the hollowed bullet and the one that's not hollowed out?" He said, "The non-hollowed one will go in and come out the same size, but the hollowed one will go in the same size but you won't get it back when it comes out!" I was like, "dang!" He put the gun and the bullets back.

My brother asked if I had seen Jr's new toy. I told him no, so Jr. showed me two knives. One was a knife that was wide and went thin to a sharp point. On the handle it had an eagle claw so the hand won't slide off the handle. The knife went over my hand. The other went over and under my hand. One knife was bigger than the other one. The big knife went over my hand like the other one, and the smaller one connected under my hand. It had finger grip to where my fingers had to be in a specific spot.

I went into Jr.'s room and I was going to lie on his bed till he told me he wanted to show me his new blanket. It was Siberian White Tiger. I saw the blanket, and folded it on the bed. We were talking to each other about what had been going on with each other in the past. We, well I, brought up the subject of what movie we were going to see. So then that's when my brother and Manny came in saying "Awww...what are you doing?" We told them, "nothing just catching up on the past." They said, "Ya right!!" So, they left room and we started to chat some more. Then they came in again and said, "I know what y'all are doing, y'all are getting busy, right?" We said no it's not like that. They asked what movie we were going to see and I said, Final Destination 2. My brother said, Darkness Falls. We were like well, what movie are we going to see? Jr. said, "We'll see both of them." We were like "all right!" So we agreed on both of them.

Well, my brother and Manny were playing with the gun in the living room. Jr. went to go see what they were chatting about so loud. He saw them with the gun and told them not to play like that. Jr. came back to the room and put the gun next to the bed while I was facing the opposite way. He rubbed my back, neck and head. I told him I had an eerie feeling in my stomach. He asked me what it was. I told him I didn't know, but what I did know was that it wasn't going to be good at all. I wanted to talk to my brother, Moses, in the other room and he said, "I have to go pee." I told him to go and come right back. Moses went to the restroom. Jr. had picked up the gun and aimed it at Manny. Manny told him to stop playing. Jr. put his finger on the trigger and BANG, the gun shot off! Right when Jr. shot the gun Manny said, "Jr. No!" Manny fell on the ground twitching. Jr. rolled back on me, his legs also came up when he shot the gun. I got up from the bed and asked, "was that a blank?' Jr. said, "No!" I panicked and told my brother, who was still in the bathroom peeing, to get out. Moses asked why. I told him that Jr. had shot Manny in the eye. Manny's eye looked like a plum. His brain was coming out of his head. There was blood coming out of his mouth, ears, nose and eye. There was a puddle of blood. He thought I was playing until he saw Manny on the floor twitching and blood coming out of his mouth and eye. Jr. didn't know what to do. He was walking back and forward from Manny to the living room. Moses and I were crying telling Manny not to die on us. I held Manny's hand and told him if he could hear me to squeeze my hand. He did for only three seconds. Moses and I were checking his pulse like we'd seen on TV, "Trauma Life in the ER." Jr. told me to hide the gun some where. He was going to give it to me and then hid it in between the sofa pillows. He told Moses to help carry Manny outside so he should at least stay alive for a while since it was cold out there. Jr. had called 9-11 two times. They finally came over and said that this was a D.O.A (Dead on Arrival.) Manny had died instantly by a 38 revolver gun at around 2:30pm, on February 8th, 2003, Saturday evening at the Stone Hollow Apartments. We were asked questions about what had happened. Jr. had made up a person so he would not get in trouble. We went along with it until we had to go to the police station. We rode in different cop cars. All three of us. The Detective said that if we didn't tell her the truth that we would be sent to prison for lying about a homicide (a murder.) We were all in separate rooms and we all had different detectives. My mom, my step sister, Estella, my little brother, Matthew, and my soon-to-be step dad, Martin, came downtown to where we were. My mom was crying. She thought one of us had been shot. She saw me and started crying a lot more and asked where Moses was and if he was alive and okay. I told her he was okay and that he was in the room behind us. She was like, "Thank God my two babies are alive and okay!" My Mom asked where Jr. was. I told her he was in the back room by the jail cells. I told her I thought they were videotaping him because he had the most blood on him. Then my brother, Moses, came out of the room and we went home and told Mom the whole story. We left the police station around 7:30pm that night. I waited for the news to come on and the story was on every news channel. My friend called me and said that the story was on channel thirteen. I was watching that channel and then out of no where me, my friend, Emilio, and my mom saw me and my brother on TV. We freaked out because we were trying so hard not to be on the news. About thirty minutes later my dad and step mom called and asked what happened, because my dad's family had called my parents and told them me and Moses were on the news. To tell you the truth, my brother and I didn't want any body to know, just us and Jr. We thought it would be better if no one knew what had happened. We didn't want any body to worry about us and say that we couldn't handle the pressure or what was going on.

What my message is, don't play with guns at all. Don't matter who you are, or what your experience is. Don't ever aim a gun to anybody if you are playing!! Doesn't matter if you have a safety or not. Be smart. You won't realize what you've done till that split second is over and your friend is on the floor bleeding, screaming and twitching.

—Rachel Sanchez, grade 11

Lesson 15:
The Onion: Unlayering What We Know

The Onion			
One (real) belief, something I know	How do I know this? (Tell one way you know)	If that had not happened, how else would you know it?	If that had not happened, how else would you know it?

We know things because we live them over and over. We might hear something once and suspect it's true, but the first time we experience it for ourselves, we know it's true. As we grow older, we experience our truths over and over, in different situations, and they become part of the fabric of what we know.

In this text structure, students trace something they know, showing how three different moments in their lives, or three different instances, add up to one truth.

Teaching *The Onion* as a Timed, Guided Writing:

(On an overhead projector, place a piece of artwork and an opinion or theme statement that correlates with a piece of literature you are reading in class. Sample: Travelers look happier at the beginning of a journey than at the end.*)*

1. Look at the artwork.
2. Copy the statement. If you don't believe it's true, change it to make it true for you.
3. For the next minute, explain the statement. (What does it mean? What is your interpretation of it?)
4. Take a breath and indent. For the next three minutes, tell one way you know it's true.
5. Take a breath and indent. Look at what you just wrote. Imagine that what you wrote had never happened. Tell another way you know the statement is true. You have three minutes.
6. Take a breath and indent. Now imagine that what you just wrote had never happened. What is one more way you would know that the statement is true?

(Share, either with partners or in large group, using volunteers.)
(Discuss any of the following.)
Does anyone have a paragraph that you consider the strongest? The weakest?
If you were going to rearrange your paragraphs, which would you want to lead with? To end with?
How could you link the incidents together to make clear transitions?
What could you do to finish the piece, without repeating anything?

Teaching *The Onion* as a Kernel Essay:

(On an overhead projector, place a piece of artwork and an opinion or theme statement that correlates with a piece of literature you are reading in class).

1. Take a look at the sentence and the artwork, students. *(Read the statement aloud. Sample:* Travelers look happier at the beginning of a journey than at the end. *)* Do you agree with it? If you do, copy it at the top of your page. Do you need to change some of the words to make it more true for you? If you do, go ahead and revise the sentence, and doing that will make it a prompt that you believe is true. Write your version at the top of your page.
   (On the blackboard or overhead, display the text structure boxes shown at the beginning of this lesson.)
2. Directly underneath the statement, copy these boxes, including the words in them.
3. Now on your paper, underneath the boxes, write one sentence to go with each of the boxes. If you'd like to draw a line from your sentence to the box, go ahead. You have about five minutes. You've already got your sentence for the first box. *(Give the students writing time.)*

(Share, either with partners or in large group, using volunteers.)

(Discuss any of the following.)

Do the sentences all "hang together"? *(Discuss the cohesiveness or need for transitions.)* Was this hard or easy? *(Discuss why.)*

Do you hear how each one of those kernel essays is just like a perfect plan for a whole essay? How any one of them could be expanded into a full-blown, wonderful essay? *(Decide with the class what to do with the essays next, whether to work on them or abandon them and move on.)*

Photo by Gloria Butler, courtesy of Brittany Martinez

121. Travelers always look happier at the beginning of a journey than at the end.

Los viajeros siempre se ven más felices cuando la jornada empieza que cuando acaba.

Freewriting Samples

Travelers always look better at the beginning of a trip than at the end. I mean, how many people do you know that after a week of hiking in the mountains come home and want to run a mile or two? I don't know anybody like that. If you do, let me know. Most people, when they get home, want to take a nap and rest.

—Hunter Sparks, grade 9

Ha! This reminds me of me and my family because when we went to Cancun, Mexico we were so happy to go but our last day when we were coming home we were all mean and tired and our faces were so different than the first day when we left.

—Jackie Dunn, grade 9

Guided Writing Samples

I know that at the beginning of a journey you are always happy, but after the trials and tribulations of the trip you are not always happy.

One way I know this is true is because my family and I always love to journey, and at the beginning we are happier than at the end.

Another way I know it is true is because my cousins went on a journey from New Mexico to our house and when they ended the trip they were tired and miserable.

Another way I know it's true is because of books. The Lord of the Rings series is all one long journey put into three books. When they start all is good and then at the end they are tired and not happy at all.

So that is my theory. Yours can be different, but I still think what I think: that people always look happier at the beginning of a journey than the end.

—Kim Goss, grade 9

Kernel Essay Samples

This is true in school. In the first and second grade all of the kids love coming to school. But then teachers start introducing more homework and harder subjects. Then kids start to hate it. After every year is over, all the kids are happy until the end of summer when they start dreading school. Then at the end of high school all the seniors are happy, but once they get out, they either go to more schooling in college or to the working world and suddenly they miss school.

—James Armstrong, grade 9

I believe that boys should never kick girls. I believe that because my brother gets in trouble for kicking me. If my brother had not kicked me, I would still believe because my friends say so. I would still believe this because my parents say so.

—Rachel, grade 4

I believe in God. I know it's true because how else would all be created? It's just faith. Faith is not seeing God, but still believing in him. Also I go to CCD. (Even if this weren't true...) I would still believe because I still go to church. My sister makes me go, even if I don't want to. I would still believe because I have my sister's picture Bible she loaned me. I naturally would want a reason.

—Marie, grade 4

Lesson 16:
The Spin of a Coin (Finding the Paradox)

The Spin of a Coin (Finding the Paradox)

Two sides of the coin		How they are true in a fiction character		How they are true in a character in history		
How the thought is true	How the opposite is also true					What strikes me as most puzzling

---

Sean Mullen, an eleventh-grade student, says, "I can't think of any one true thing that doesn't have an opposite that is also true." He's on to something: paradoxes permeate our lives. How easy is it to think up a paradox? Incredibly easy. All you have to do is think up something true, and then consider its opposite, and voilà! A paradox.

For example, friends can give you support. The opposite? Friends can hurt you. When students consider these two sides of the coin, then they are ready to also consider how the two sides operate in various situations, in literature, or in their lives. What results is more interesting discourse, layered with complexity.

More sophisticated thinkers and writers compare relationships to other relationships, to inspect the dynamics and analogies between the parts. This structure invites that kind of thinking and can provide interesting mental gymnastics for writers.

Teaching *The Spin of a Coin* as a Timed, Guided Writing:

(On an overhead projector, place a piece of artwork and an opinion or theme statement that correlates with a piece of literature you are reading in class. Sample: We are guided by those who have gone before us.*)*

1. Look at the artwork.
2. Copy the statement.
3. For the next minute, explain the statement. (What does it mean? What is your interpretation of it?)
4. What do you think the opposite of the statement would be? *(Talk over a possible opposite, and settle on one as a class. For example:* We have to guide ourselves; *or:* We can be misguided by those who have gone before us; *or:* We are guided more by those around us now.*)* Write that statement down, and explain it for the next minute.

5. Take a breath and indent. You have written two sides of the same coin. Think about how those two sides of the coin are both true for a character in a piece of literature you've read, a story. Explain it in the next three minutes.
6. Take a breath and indent. Think about how those two sides of the coin are true for a character in history. You have three minutes.
7. Take a breath and indent one more time. Read over what you've said in your discussion. Think of one thing about this paradox that puzzles you. Write down what the thing is that puzzles you. You have one minute.

(Share, either with partners or in large group, using volunteers.)
(Discuss any of the following.)
Was this like mental juggling?
Do you hear how much more complex your thinking is in these pieces? How do you explain that?
Can you think of any other categories you'd like to use besides literature and history?
What about how the paradox works in your personal lives?
Is this a structure you could imagine using?

Teaching *The Spin of a Coin* as a Kernel Essay:

(On an overhead projector, place a piece of artwork and an opinion or theme statement that correlates with a piece of literature you are reading in class. Sample: We are guided by those who have gone before us.*)*

1. Take a look at the sentence and the artwork, students. *(Read the statement aloud.)* Do you agree with it? If you do, copy it at the top of your page. Do you need to change some of the words to make it more true for you? If you do, go ahead and revise the sentence, and doing that will make it a prompt that you believe is true. Write your version at the top of your page.
    (On the blackboard or overhead, display the text structure boxes shown at the beginning of this lesson.)
2. Directly underneath the statement, copy these boxes, including the words in them.
3. Now on your paper, underneath the boxes, write one sentence to go with each of the boxes. If you'd like to draw a line from your sentence to the box, go ahead. You have about five minutes. You may need to change the words in the original sentence as you write. *(Give the students writing time.)*

(Share, either with partners or in large group, using volunteers.)
(Discuss any of the following.)
What do you think of what you heard?
Were the pieces easy to follow? *(Discuss the cohesiveness or need for transitions.)*
Was this more difficult than other structures you've used? *(Discuss why.)*
We used the analogy relationship "opposites" here. Are there other analogy relationships that we could use in a structure?
(Decide with the class what to do with the essays next, whether to work on them or abandon them and move on.)

Photo courtesy of US NPS

090. We are guided by all those who have gone before us.
Somos guiados por todos aquellos que han pasado antes que nosotros.

Kernel Essay Samples

The world needs some bad people to make it more fun. But the world should never ever argue or fight because it would be much easier to live. Jade (Jackie Chan Adventures) would be very disappointed and bored if there wasn't anyone to fight off. I think it is fun to argue over certain subjects and be competitive. Martin Luther King Jr. wanted world peace, but I bet he wouldn't mind arguing every once in a while. What's puzzling about this is that I love to argue, but I get so exasperated with the extra stubborn ones, I say, "Whatever," and go away.
—Maria, grade 4

Guidance is what makes people, a person or a nation strong. Although we do not know who or what is guiding us, there is no way to follow.

In history, from the first, our nation was, and still is, guided by the constitution that the people stand by. Although in the breaking away from England and wading out on our own, we had to walk blindly in order to make a path.

In The Odyssey, Odysseus was guided by the Gods, until he was almost taken over by Poseidon, Lord of the sea.

In actuality we are guided by our lights; the people we see before our eyes or the person we see ourselves to be. Many times we are the light guiding those behind us.
—Jessica McCall, grade 9

Lesson 17:
Tevye's Debate

Tevye's Debate

On one hand	On the other hand	But on the other hand	But on the other hand	How can I be guided when the choice is so tough

Sometimes people come to a point in their lives where a course of action isn't clear-cut. What do we do in those situations? We do what Tevye did, in Fiddler on the Roof: we mull over the "what-ifs" on both sides of the issue. This structure allows the student's thought to wander back and forth, mulling over a thought, considering first one side and then the other. The results can be surprising and thoughtful.

Teaching *Tevye's Debate* as a Timed, Guided Writing:

Have you ever seen the play *Fiddler on the Roof*? In it, the main character, Tevye, debates about what to do. He constantly seems to say "on the one hand" and later, "on the other hand." He constantly argues with himself about pros and cons. Let's try his way.
(On an overhead projector, place a piece of artwork and an opinion or theme statement that correlates with a piece of literature you are reading in class. Sample: People have different kinds of goals.*)*

1. Look at the artwork, and let's read the statement. Do you agree with it? If you do, copy it at the top of your page. Do you feel an urge to change it? Go ahead. One student rewrote it like this: "Everyone should have a cat." Feel free to specify any kind of goal you think people should have, if you like. Write your version at the top of your page. You have two minutes to get a sentence you believe. *(Give the students two minutes' thinking/writing time.)*
2. Now, right after your statement, explain it. You have two minutes.
3. Now take a breath and indent. Write the words "On the other hand," and for the next two minutes talk about how the opposite is true.
4. Take a breath and indent. Start with the words "But on the other hand," and switch back to the first point of view. Don't repeat yourself, but think of new ways to say what's true.

Teaching *Tevye's Debate* as a Kernel Essay:

(On an overhead projector, place a piece of artwork and an opinion or theme statement that correlates with a piece of literature you are reading in class. Sample: People have different kinds of goals.*)*

1. Take a look at the sentence and the artwork, students. *(Read the statement aloud.)* Do you agree with it? If you do, copy it at the top of your page. Do you need to change some of the words to make it more true for you? If you do, go ahead and revise the sentence, and doing that will make it a prompt which you believe is true. Write your version at the top of your page.
(On the blackboard or overhead, display the text structure boxes shown at the beginning of this lesson.)
2. Directly underneath the statement, copy these boxes, including the words in them.
3. Now on your paper, underneath the boxes, write one sentence to go with each of the boxes. If you'd like to draw a line from your sentence to the box, go ahead. You have about five minutes. You've already got your sentence for the first box.
(Give the students writing time.)
(Share, either with partners or in large group, using volunteers.)
Does your back-and-forth discussion sound genuine? *(Discuss the cohesiveness or need for transitions.)*
Was it hard not to repeat yourself? *(Discuss why.)*
Do you hear how each one of those kernel essays is just like a perfect plan for a whole essay? How any one of them could be expanded into a full, thoughtful essay?
What kind of evidence would you put into the parts? *(Decide with the class what to do with the essays next, whether to work on them or abandon them and move on.)*

Photo by Gretchen Bernabei

160. People have different kinds of goals.
La gente tiene diferentes metas.

Truism Samples

Truisms by fourth graders from looking at the photo:

Everyone has a goal. —Jacob

Nothing's like that first goal. —Sallie

Nothing's impossible if you look at it from a different angle. —Justin

Goals will take you to your future. —Anthony

The day doesn't last forever. —Hillary

Kernel Essay Samples

I think everyone should have a cat because they are cute. I think everyone should not have a cat because they mess up your house sometimes. I think everyone needs a cat because Sylvester is cute. But Tweety Bird would be scared a lot. Ally loves them. I don't think people should have cats because I hate them. What's puzzling to me is why people want cats and others don't.
—Rachel, grade 4

On one hand, as a child all you have to worry about is being cute and hoping you don't wet the bed (big burden). On the other hand, as a teen you have to worry about grades and peer pressure. But on the other hand, as an adult you have to worry about money and how you are going to pay the bills. All stages of life have their troubles.
—Kyle Carillo, grade 9

The tardy policy at O'Connor is strict. There are a lot of things that you can not avoid that would get you a tardy, like going to the bathroom or traffic on the way to school.

But people have started to get to class on time. During passing periods there seem to be less people standing around talking, so it's easier to get to class.

Sometimes though there are times that I am late and the teachers don't catch me in the hall and give me a tardy but the teacher whose class I am going to makes me go get a tardy slip which kind of ticks me off. Really though I should have tried harder to get to class faster, like ran or gotten a pass from my last period teacher.

The tardy policy is a good policy I suppose, as long as it had boundaries. Going to the bathroom and getting a 4th tardy so you have to go to detention. Then it's just like you don't want to go to the bathroom and so you hold it all day.

Really if something has boundaries and has an obvious point and it works, I will support it. This has little boundaries though. Because of this, I still don't like it.
—Russell, grade 11

Full Essay Sample

June 5, 20xx - Dear Journal,

Man that sounds so hokey. "Dear Journal." I hate this. Mom's making me write a stupid journal for the summer. Of course, getting busted for weed earlier this week didn't put me in Ma's good graces. As punishment she's making me get in that dorky Big Brother/Big Sister program. Good bye summer, hello hell. I can picture my summer getting flushed down the toilet. No more friends; no more parties. This totally bites! Ah! I mean, I got caught with a little bit of weed, not a kilo. I told Mom, "You know that if Dad was here, I wouldn't be in trouble." She always yells back about how Dad was a loser and how I should never want to be like him. Well, how about this for a journal entry. I can't do this forever.

Jun 12, 20xx - Dear Journal,

This whole journal things becoming OK. I hope my friends never read this. I met Rick today for the second time. He's in his twenties, which would normally make him cool, but he's all religious and stuff. I can't stand that dogma junk. It makes me sick. I don't want to think about it any more. I'm sneaking out the window, probably aught to hide this journal.

Jun 30, 20xx - Dear Journal,

All I can think about is Rick; the guy from Big Brothers. I want to stop thinking about what he said because it makes me weak and sick to my stomach. I was starting to get to like him. He didn't seem so religious the last few times, and he was blaring rock music in his car as he drove me to the movies. On the way back, though, he started talking about God and all the other stuff. I can hardly think straight. I think I'm going to go read that book he gave me since I'm grounded to the house. He called it a 'bible' or something. I don't remember. Oh well.

July 28, 20xx - Dear Journal,

Rick was taking me to me downtown yesterday when I saw some of my old friends. They were smoking blunts and drinking in an alley. I wish I would have asked Rick to stop so that I could talk to them about God and how I've changed. Life is great. I can't stop thinking about things and ideas and I love it. Well, I would like to write more, but I have to go to church. Thankfully Mom's coming this time. It's so wonderful. Laters.

—Brad A. Ballinger, grade 10

3

Experimenting with Thick Description

Design Your Frame

> *Everything means, is understood, as a part of a greater whole—there is a constant interaction between meanings, all of which have the potential of conditioning others…This dialogic imperative . . . insures that there can be no actual monologue.*
> —Mikhail Bakhtin, *The Dialogic Imagination*

No actual monologue. There can be no actual monologue? Well, sure, maybe in the world, in the hallways and cafeterias, wherever humans gather, but what about in academia? in writing? Aren't traditional essays monologues on paper?

Our students are bored with essays, as are we, because monologues just don't exist in our real lives. Five-paragraph essays, and constraining, formulaic writing of all kinds, truly are an alien life form, nowhere to be found in the natural world. A state trooper doesn't talk to speeding motorists in five paragraphs. (It would be hilarious if one did.) Waitstaff taking dinner orders don't deliver monologues to their patrons, except maybe briefly when they're performing "today's specials." Business dealings? Phone calls? Movie scenes? Whispers in movie theaters? Nah. It's all dialogues, many different kinds of dialogues.

Maybe Bakhtin is right. Maybe all human discourse, all human communication, is constant interaction. What if we applied this dialogic imperative to essays? What if we considered essays to be, at the very least, one side of a dialogue?

The question for teachers, then, is how do we create forms that reflect multiple voices, while still accomplishing the goals of an essay? What would forms look like if they're not monologues? Nonmonological? How in the world do we teach that?

Musing on these questions, I thought about an article I wrote for The English Journal, an article that was almost entirely dialogue. What had shaped that form for me had been the wording in the call for manuscripts:

> The heart of the "case" consists of what ethnographers call "thick description"; i.e., anecdotes, transcripts or reconstructed dialogue, writing samples, contextual details, field notes, and the like.

Field notes. Ethnographers. Were we talking about Dian Fossey types who studied gorillas and logged their moves? I did some reading. Ethnographers, I learned, study and record human cultures. The more I read, the more I was reminded of what my students routinely record in their journals: verbatim conversations, favorite songs, copies of poems, photographs, movie tickets, ads they're answering, notes from friends, snippets of language from their lives, and candy wrappers, graduation invitations, photocopies of first driver's licenses, graphics depicting nonverbal, meaningful moments. Life texts. Their own personal field notes as observers of their lives. Field notes recording themselves as participants in their lives. In their journals, are students the ethnographer or the subject under study? Or both?

I found answers about thick description in Clifford Geertz's *The Interpretation of Cultures*, in a discussion about winking. Consider one person winking at another. A thin description of that action would sound like "a brief contraction of one eyelid, whereby the muscles cause the lower part of the eyelid to touch the lower eyelashes." Thick description might sound like "a nervous twitch," or "a wink, letting you in on a practical joke in progress." Thin description offers field notes as mechanical, superficial description without any interpretation; thick description offers field notes with enough social and cultural context to make the meaning clear.

I decided to try it out on my thirteen-year-old daughter.

Me: Matilde, watch this. *(With my face otherwise completely impassive, I slowly closed my left eye and then opened it again.)* What did I just do?

Matilde: You winked at me.

Me: What did it mean?

Matilde: I don't know. It could've been a friendly kind of wink, a flirty kind of wink, a joking kind of wink. I don't know.

Me: Why don't you know?

Matilde: Well…for me…I'd need something like a sentence before it and after it. Then I'd know.

Later, I asked Matilde, "What kind of sentence, before?"
She answered, "We sold your cat in a garage sale." (Joking kind.) "Hi." (Friendly kind.) "You're lookin' good…" (Flirty kind.)

Matilde demonstrated for me the complex, contextualized nature of human signs and signals we read every day. We use language to get clues about how to make sense out of our observations, our "field notes." Over time, our values and beliefs form, and they rise from layers and layers of interactions with members of our many groups. Yet when it comes to assigning essays, we have traditionally taught "academic" writing to exclude the richness of how we got to be the way we are, and to include instead some pretty thin description. I know I have.

If my *English Journal* introduction to the powers of thick description didn't cause me to snap in 1991 (see the introduction), then Harvey Daniels's voice in my ear should have in 2002. In "Expository Text in Literature Circles" from the May 2002 *Voices from the Middle*, Daniels looks at the way we teach expository writing, in pure forms:

- cause/effect
- compare/contrast
- pro/con
- problem/solution
- definition/categorization
- order/sequence/procedure
- description/listing

Yep, those sound like the kinds of nonfiction we learned in school, and which we have taught. Then Daniels examines several newspaper stories. Lo and behold, they are full of dialogue, characters, vignettes, sounds, images. It's no surprise to us as readers that real-world nonfiction does not stick to pure textbook expository forms any more than real-world driveway-moment-type essays stick to a five-paragraph essay formula. No! They're full of all the elements of fiction. They're full of all the elements, I'm recognizing now, of really engaging field notes. Thick description.

> As we read further into these three articles, we find much more complex, diverse, and recursive organizational patterns than the trusty old curriculum guides led us to expect. There is a welter of structures used in each piece, with the authors seeming to slide between one and another, a paragraph at a time, without warning. After an opening vignette, there might be a paragraph listing some items of import, followed by another vignette, told chronologically; then there might be the posing of a problem and some possible solutions, followed by a sequence of past events, a list of examples just piled on top of each other, and then still more narrative. All these articles seem to be organizational hybrids; nothing is simple or straightforward. (9)

Mixing forms together can create something new and powerful. Have you seen the publisher Dorling Kindersley's *Eyewitness Classics* series? They're gorgeous. The complete texts of classic stories like *Black Beauty* and *Robin Hood* are presented to readers, surrounded by little illustrated factoids all around each page. VH1's *Popup Videos*, incredibly popular with our students, present songs with embedded biographical details about the band members. Sandra Cisneros's recent book *Caramelo* interweaves conversation with story in an innovative way. It's a madcap, genre-bending world.

In *Illuminating Texts*, Jim Burke points to the new ways of reading in the digital age:

> Authors' increasing attention to the design, format, and structure of a text, whether on the screen or on the page, will demand that readers know how to skim, scan, screen—and just plain read, of course. Everything in our accelerated society points toward faster living and greater distraction—and, thus, the need to read well on the run (3).

If readers are more and more attracted to reading multiple kinds of text in the same piece, how do we teach writers to write those same kinds of pieces?

Nancie Atwell showed us years ago in *In the Middle* how to teach struggling writers to write effective leads, using dialogue, action, and thoughts. For many of us, that's where the play stopped in our assignments, and the resulting student pieces looked like five-paragraph essays with really engaging leads. Our student writers are ready for more.

With these thoughts in mind, we can experiment with various kinds of thick description, or meaningful texts from our lives, possible texts that ethnographers would consider field notes:

- dialogue
- lyrics
- sound effects
- thoughts or inner dialogues
- descriptions
- images
- anecdotes
- recognizable or familiar historical, sacred, or scientific texts
- meaningful or symbolic objects

Where does thick description go? What are the possibilities? As a beginning, writers can experiment with using any of the above kinds of thick description in the following ways, within the text of an essay. Let's take lyrics as an example, and trace it through the following:

- *Framing.* Think of a picture frame. The writer would use one of the forms of thick description to begin and end the piece. Maybe one stanza of a song for the beginning, and another stanza for the ending.

- *Ribboning.* Think of a girl's hair braided with a ribbon in the braid, the color of the ribbon disappearing and reappearing. The writer would use one of the forms of thick description in the same way, throughout the piece. For example, one line of the lyrics may begin the piece, then a paragraph or so later, another line of the lyrics, and so on until the end.

- *Weaving.* Weave your fingers together and look at them. The writer would do the same with similar proportions of text and thick description. (See student samples with woven lyrics in the next lesson.)

- *Echoes.* Think of how a song can run through your mind, even when you're talking to someone else. The writer would allow some recurring thick description to echo throughout a text. (For example, the lyrics might have a line repeated for echo effect, where it doesn't get repeated in the actual song.)

- *Embedding.* Thick description can be embedded right into the text, and not separated from it. (The text would actually mention the lyrics, not juxtapose them in any way; for example, in a narrative, one of the characters might sing the song. Or talk about it.)

What's it supposed to look like? Give students visual models (like the samples that follow), or they will never realize that you're giving them permission to step away from the five-paragraph look.

As you try these ideas with students, keep a sharp eye out for the students who "do it wrong" or different from your vision. "No, that's not what I meant" can become "Hey, let's see how that works when you read it out loud." That's the way to find lessons, through the possibilities in accidental inventions.

Lesson 18:
Lullabye Weave

What would happen if a writer wove together two completely different kinds of text? What if you wove together a memory, along with lyrics from a lullabye? In this twenty-minute exercise, writers will freewrite two short pieces, then follow structured directions to form a third piece from their two original pieces. Thick description woven into prose creates something breathtaking. This short, twenty-minute exercise demonstrates the simplicity and power of using not only descriptions of our memories, but also the actual text that has the power to transport us to those memories. If something so powerful can happen in a tiny exercise, it will follow that similar kinds of text-weaving, used judiciously in an essay, could create something truly wonderful. Samples follow the instructions.

Teaching It:

Try this out with me, and let's see what happens.

First, take a sheet of paper. Draw a horizontal line across the middle of the paper, separating the top from the bottom. Keep the bottom half empty. Now, look at the top half. Divide it in half with a vertical line. It should look like this. *(Show a page divided as you described; see sample below.)*

Now, think of a song you remember someone singing to you. It might be a lullabye, or a Broadway show tune, or any kind of song at all. The important thing is that you remember someone singing it to you when you were little. *(It might also be something they said, like a nursery rhyme, or a saying; the important thing is that you remember the sound of someone saying it to you.)*

In the top right section, write the words to the song, about four lines. More if you can remember. Write them in poetry form, not paragraph form. *(Give them a few minutes.)*

Now, think of the person whose voice that was, and how they looked if you could have taken a snapshot of them, at a time they might have been singing (or saying) those words to you. On the left side of the top, write a paragraph, describing them as clearly as you can, so that we can picture them as you do in your mind's eye. Were they sitting? On what? What did their eyes look like? What do you remember most about how they looked? What might have been going on at that time? *(Give them a few minutes.)*

Look at the lines on the right. Number every line, using ONLY even numbers. *(2, 4, 6, 8...)*

Look at the paragraph on the left. Underline five or six phrases that are the most important (the best phrases, or words) in the paragraph. *(Wait a minute.)* Now number the underlined phrases, using odd numbers (1, 3, 5, 7...)

Now the work is all done! Look at my fingers. *(Hold up your two hands, fingers outstretched and palms out, and demonstrate slowly merging your fingers together.)* That's what we're going to do. *(Repeat the slow demonstration.)* All you need to do is reshape the numbered parts into the shape of a poem, in the space on the bottom of the page. Start by copying line one first. Directly underneath it, copy line two. Continue until you're finished.

Feel free to repeat any lines you want to, to make it come out evenly.

(Give them time to complete it.)

Could we hear how they sound now? *(Partner-share, and then hear a few in large-group share.)* When you read aloud, read them very slowly.

Debriefing Questions:

Did you hear any that "got you"?

What made them so effective?

Did you hear any that didn't work at all?

Was anyone surprised at what happened, how it sounded, when you wove the two together?

Spin-offs:

Try weaving together a situation from your memory along with a discussion of a theme like the sample by Kelsey Hall.
Try variations of the columns by including:
• Lines from a love song/description of a sweetheart from that time
• Famous lines from speeches/descriptions of leadership
• Lines from a popular song when you were younger/description of your best friend from then

Try a dialogue as one of the columns, then weave snippets from it into prose.
Try significant lines of text from a piece of literature as one of the columns, and first-person character analysis on the other.

Lullaby Weave Sample:

I grew up at my Grandma and Pop-pop's house. From Elizabeth, my nickname was Betsy, which morphed into "Bitsy." 1 I was the smallest person in the house! 3 Nearly everyone who lived there or visited worked in Pop-pop's garden 5 (except for Aunt Kay, but that's a story for another time!). It was nearly two acres and grew some of my most favorite things . . . sweet corn, strawberries, cucumbers and a Queen Anne cherry tree. 7 With all those people around, I got quite a bit of attention, being so short and all. And EVERYONE sang that silly song to me. That song could be heard coming from every corner of the house. 9 It could be heard coming from the rows of the garden in the gravelly, Pennsylvania-accented voice of my Pop-pop. 11 I can still see my mother's hands.

Itsy Bitsy spider went up the waterspout 2

Down came the rain and washed the spider out 4

Out came the sun and dried up all the rain 6

Then Itsy Bitsy spider went up the spout again. 8

My nickname was Betsy, which morphed into Bitsy.
Itsy Bitsy Spider went up the waterspout
I was the smallest person in the house!
Down came the rain and washed the spider out.
Nearly everyone who lived there or visited worked in Pop-pop's garden.
Out came the sun and dried up all the rain.
It grew some of my most favorite things . . .
Sweet corn
Strawberries
Cucumbers
A Queen Anne cherry tree
Then Itsy Bitsy spider went up the spout again.
That song could be heard coming from every corner of the house
And from the rows of the garden in the gravelly, Pennsylvania-accented voice of
My Pop-pop
Itsy Bitsy spider . . .

—Liz Ozuna, Teacher

Sample Woven Poems:

Mom

Talented at singing, sewing, talking
Amazing grace, how sweet the sound
Comfortable to snuggle with
That saved a wretch like me,
Swedish, Irish, righteousness
I once was lost
Caring, mom to two
But now I am found
Brown, curly hair, blue eyes,
Was blind
Eyes in the back of her head
But now I see
My mom

—Katrina Armstrong, Grade 3

My Brother

My brother is very humorous
One
He loves to play with me
Two
He loves to see his family laugh
Three
He thinks in a different way
Four
When my brother first heard Say Shava Shava
Say Shava Shava Ahines
Without seeing the movie Kubhi Kushi Kubhi Ghum
Say Shava Shava Ahines
He thought the song was about a man
Say Shava Shava Ahines
Who did a crime and was going to get punished.
He thought Shava meant punish. He is the best brother.
Say Shava Shava Ya!

—Vikram Parolkar, Grade 4

Tea Pot

I'm a little tea pot
When I fell off my roof
short and stout
I was crying and cut my leg.
here is my handle
my mom started singing this
this is my spout
song to make me laugh. While,
When I get steamed up
she was cleaning my cut with
hear me shout
alcohol and putting a bandaid
tip me over
on my knee
and pour me out.

—Jason Criollo, grade 11

Sample Woven Essay

We All Make It Through

I remember being downstairs and playing on my new Nintendo, when I heard the phone ring.
Everything fell silent.

" 'Are you awake, Emily? Can I get you something?'... 'No, I'm all right, go back to sleep, Mother' " (809). So many of us, like Emily in "I Stand Here Ironing," by Tillie Olsen, suppress our feelings for many different reasons. Whether it be fear, shame, confusion, or just to keep our loved ones from worry, we are all guilty of it.

Hardships are a part of life that no one can escape. Everyday in life, we learn our most important lessons from living through and seeing others living through their hardships. Depending on the soul of the person, everyone deals with hard times differently. Many people suppress their emotions, while others allow their feeling to pour out. I can't explain why others deal with them harder than some, but I do know that we all in the end make it through a rough time only stronger for having lived it.

The only thing I could comprehend out of the confusion that I felt was the cries and tears pouring out of my sister and the running footsteps I heard as my mom raced down the stairs. She told me nothing other than the simple fact that my Grandma was at the hospital. I sat there and listened to the garage close, and wondered if I'd ever see her again.

In The Crucible by Arthur Miller, many hardships are lived out by the characters. After losing his dignity in front of the whole town when revealing that he had known Abigail, and after leading his married life a lie, John Proctor decides to go down with pride. When asked to sign to it that he had dealings with the Devil, he said, "I am not worth the dust on the feet of them that hang" (240). He knows he's lived a bad life. The end of the last scene with Elizabeth and John is very passionate yet full of sorrow. After making it through the hardship of John's infidelity, now Elizabeth must cope with the fact that she will never see him again. She was one whose emotions and feelings poured out. Her husband was about to die, and although the script doesn't blatantly tell us that she came out stronger, the last line leaves us good reason to believe that she did.

Elizabeth said, barely able to hold herself up and through tears, "He have his goodness now. God forbid I take it from him" (240). Now that John finally had something honorable to back his name, she was content, even though it meant his death.

Another example of a hardship from a piece of literature is in the article "Being Shot at is No Fun," by Wayne Downing. In it he talks about the war in Vietnam, and says, "Like many other soldiers who have been in combat, I have spent a lifetime trying to suppress many of my memories and feelings about the traumatic events that I experienced on the battlefield" (141). In his situation, his reasoning for not bringing forth his feelings and memories was for lack of wanting to re-visit and remember the battlefield at Vietnam.

I remember seeing my Dad's truck pull up to the house with the blue barrels in the bed. He had just returned from the ranch, and just then we heard the heartbreaking sound of the phone ring again. My sister answered it and without saying a word handed it to my dad. For a thirteen year old, I was pretty perceptive on people and their time and expressions. I knew the news was bad.

She was gone.

Kendall cried until she had nothing left to cry. I, on the other hand, cried a few tears and then like I always do, went and sat in my bed and just thought. I've always kept my problems inside and Kendall has always let them out.

My family came out stronger and now we can look back on the good times we had with her and smile and laugh. Whether it be losing touch with a friend, losing someone to a death, or simply going through a personal hardship, we all have them. In life we have them to become stronger.

For what doesn't kill us, makes us stronger.

—Kelsey Hall, grade 11

Lesson 19:
Sound Effects

Skilled writers use words not only to paint images, but also to create sounds. The cry of an eagle. The sound of applause. The lonesome wind. Sounds like these can take a reader deep into an experience with very few words. How does this work?

Activating the senses evokes that "tacit knowing" that defies logic. Yet beginning writers don't often feel empowered to craft sound effects through their words.

In this exercise, students practice their skills at choosing, crafting, and placing the sounds of their lives to bring us to the meanings they choose to convey. They also practice putting words to intangible entities, sounds.

The only required resource would be CDs or tapes of sound effects, or .wav files, downloadable. (Professional audio libraries are especially inexpensive in used CD stores.)

Teaching It:

(Give students an index card, and get audio ready to play.)
I'm going to play for you a sound effect, and I'd like for you to listen to it twice. Don't say anything; just listen to it and think about what moment in your life it reminds you of.

(Play one, twice. I use something like a ball bouncing or a door slamming.)
Raise your hand if you would like to tell what moment from your life it reminded you of. *(Let a few students share.)*
Those were all different moments, and powerful ones.
Now listen to a different sound, and think about what moment from your life it reminds you of. I'll play it twice. After you hear it, write down on the index card what moment it reminds you of.

(Play another one, like the sound of a car starting and driving off. Give the students about two minutes to write, then share.)
Isn't it amazing how a sound is so powerful to take us right to moments in our lives?

Now, look at your writing. Look at your main idea, or the theme that you're conveying. You chose that theme because you know it, because it haunts you, because you have experience with it. Turn the card over, and write down your main idea, or your main theme of the piece. *(Share a few to make sure they have it.)*

Think of sound effects that would take a reader to that experience, or to that feeling. Now, under the place where you wrote your theme, see if you can list three or four sounds that would do the trick. For example, if your theme is about injustice, the sound might be what? Maybe a judge's gavel banging? Maybe heavy jail doors clanging shut? Give it a try, and see what you come up with.

(*Give students a couple of minutes, and then share.*)

Now, what do you do with those sounds in your paper? You can decide. Try starting the paper with sounds, ending with sounds, repeating the sounds through the middle, see what works.
(*Show students the sample.*)

Debriefing Questions:

Did you have a difficult time thinking of sounds?

Did hearing other students' sounds give you ideas you hadn't thought of yet?

Are you surprised at what happened to your paper when you added sounds?

Spin-offs:

1. Try using variations of the same sound throughout the paper (a door creaking, door slamming, a lock clicking) to help echo movement through a piece.

2. Use a series of sounds to help students create a list of memories to write about.

Sample Woven Essay, Using Sound Effects

People Could Always Use a Hug

You hear the footsteps of the girl you love, walking away.
And you hear complete silence.
When you're hurt or sad, you need a hug. Even when people are not hurt in any way, they can use a hug to make them feel better about themselves. I think everyone can use a hug in good and bad times.
I wish someone would tell me why these things happen. Why me? What did I do wrong?
One day, I thought everything was great. My girlfriend called me (I had been with her for five months). She had decided she didn't want to be with me, she said. For that whole week, I needed all the hugs I could get from best friends, good cousins, and anyone else.
"She hurt me!"
"Are you okay?"
"I don't know."
You hear the footsteps of the girl you love, walking away.
Complete silence.
—Lanze Stapleton, grade 10

Sample Conclusion With and Without Embedded Sound Effects

Without sound effects:

Alienating one man/woman for any reason should be against human ethics. Unfortunately for so many out there, alienating someone just happens to be human instinct. We discreetly do it without even realizing it. Sometimes being alone, emotionally estranged from everyone else can be the most damaging and hurtful thing to do to someone. In Lord of the Flies by William Golding and Frankenstein by Mary Shelley, these authors successfully express the physical and emotional hardships of being alienated from the rest of the world. However, in Frankenstein alienation is felt by more characters with varied situations, while in Lord of the Flies the circumstances surrounding the alienated characters are consistent among them. I hope that with my help you can easily see that.

With sound effects:

Alienating one man/woman for any reason should be against human ethics. Unfortunately for so many out there, alienating someone just happens to be human instinct. We discreetly do it without even realizing it. Sometimes being alone, emotionally estranged from everyone else can be the most damaging and hurtful thing to do to someone. Imagine being that new student. It's lunchtime, the most favorite time of the day for all students, right? For a new student, however, the cold, harsh reality of aloneness is at its worst. While the beating of your heart echoes through your ears, and your cheeks, flushed with humiliation, are seething, the sounds around you, small portions of a conversation which you long to be a part of, is the most deafening sound of all.
—Melissa Saber, grade 10

For classroom duplication only. Enlarge at 121% for 81/2 x 11 sheet

Reviving The Essay © 2005 Discover Writing Press • www.discoverwriting.com

Sample Essay with Embedded Sound Effect:

Sometimes It's Hard to Tell That Parents Want the Best for Their Children.

I remember when I lived in the Caciano Courts, a gutter, a place where it's survival of the fittest. To be more understanding, you either learn to survive at a young age, or you die at a young age. People used to think that if you were a kid growing up in Caciano Courts, you were pretty much raising yourself and I won't lie, it felt like it.

Imagine running all around the neighborhood without thinking, "Man, when are your parents gonna call," without wondering what time it is. Imagine hearing gunshots, tha tha tha!!!, and people screaming with whatever energy they have to spare. People screaming at the top of their lungs, "Help Me, I've been shot!"

And hearing, "We couldn't save your son or daughter, sorry."

Imagine them lying there in an alley and thinking to yourself that some day that could be you; your parents are at work and can't protect you. They can't just get out of work like they do today, because back then there wasn't a whole lot of money, and they had to work hard to support you.

Tell me, what's the biggest picture you can get out of that? Not much, or nothing at all, except for the fact that if you were at least twelve, you'd better have someone, and I mean someone good, to look up to or get your back when needed. It may sound sad, but honestly back then, you had to be in a gang if you didn't want to get picked on. Gangs back then were considered a way of survival in the Caciano Courts.

When I think back, it kind of feels like people were right when they said parents didn't do enough sometimes. It was hard to tell sometimes that parents only wanted the best for their children. Then I think of everything my mom's gone through to keep me alive, and how hard it was to grow up in the courts. I've come up with this fact: It doesn't matter how much you see your parents, because the truth is, the less you see your parents, because they're always at work, the more it means they love you. So I've come to believe that parents only want what's best for their children, but it's HARD to make ends meet.

—Jacob Saldivar, grade 11

For classroom duplication only. Enlarge at 121% for 81/2 x 11 sheet

Reviving The Essay © 2005 Discover Writing Press • www.discoverwriting.com   **103**

Sample Essay, Using Sound Effects as a Frame:

Got Strength?

The silence is deafening. It seems like I am in a dark hole. I can't see anything. I see a little light and start to hear some sounds. But then I remember my world feels ended but it still goes on all around. I look around the room and wake up from this dream, but it isn't a dream. My world is not what it seems. Everyone around me is happy and laughing, not knowing what goes on in my life.

People are faced with hardships throughout their rollercoaster ride of a life. Ups and downs are a part of living. Humans deal with hardships differently. How we deal with these shows how strong we can be.

Four – an age of obliviousness. An age of not knowing exactly what is going on around you. But I saw. "I lay in bed and looked at the ceiling above me and cried, thinking "where is my daddy!" My family was faced with a hard time. But we became strong and worked together. We are still a family today because of our strength. I feel that if we would have given up and become weak, our lives would have crumbled and it would have been two families instead of one.

Years passed and I was ten. A hard time then was fighting with friends and having everyone not like you. Much like Mary Warren turning to John Proctor, trying to get out of telling the truth. She had strength for a brief moment. But it shattered soon after the girls looked at her with scorn in their eyes. "Let me go, Mr. Proctor, I cannot, I cannot" (219). If I had more people backing me up when no one liked me, it wouldn't have bothered me as much as it would have if I didn't, because I would feel alone. I believe that when you have no one to help support you in certain situations, you will lose strength more easily than if you have support all around you. But the hard times I went through were candy, compared to the ones I would go through six years later.

Sweet sixteen. Is this age really sweet? Is this age easy? Of course it isn't! Yes, it can be fun, but it isn't anywhere near easy.

I opened my eyes and saw my uncle and father moving about. I thought and just knew she was gone. My strength left me. How would I deal with losing her? I cried and I cried. My grandmother was a strong woman and I think her strength rubbed off on me. The day following her death, I woke up and took long, deep breaths. I told myself I would get on with my life for her. I think her death was preparing me for the one that would soon come three months after.

Benjamen Schraer was a very good friend to my two best friends. Mickey said he was her hero, and Leska was in love with him. I met him at Leska's birthday party. He treated me as if he had known me for five years when it had only been a short five minutes. Later that night we went to Nightmare on Grayson. I walked through the haunted house not knowing what would pop out next. I saw him in front of me and felt his hand in mine and knew that if anything did pop out, I would be safe.

Five days later, I was in private singing lessons in choir. Mickey stood there in tears and said, "Ben was in an accident and they can't stop the bleeding...he's not going to make it, Sam!!"

Those words shot through me like bullets, making me weak all over. Was this possible, I asked myself over and over again. I was talking and laughing with him only five days before. I knew my grandmother was going to die, and it was only a matter of time. However, Ben's death was so sudden and unexpected. Mickey called me that night to tell me Ben did die. But I became as strong as an oak tree, because I knew my friends were in desperate need of me. I went to Mickey's house and held her. Leska came over a little while later and burst into tears, making it intensely hard for me not to break down. I didn't fall to shambles in this situation but stood strong.

The author of "Being Shot at is No Fun" made it clear that he was strong in situations as well. "Responsibility and action usually gave me no time to be afraid" (41). He was in the middle of war and had men to keep safe, as I felt I had to keep my friends safe. However, John Proctor became weak in The Crucible; when temptation was sent his way by Abby, he collapsed and gave in to her. "I know how you clutched my back behind your house and sweated like a stallion whenever I come near" (177). People have many different ways of dealing with times that are hard.

In the future, I am in fear of times that I will destroy my family's life more than mine. I am scared to possibly be laid off from a job and not be able to provide for my family. My father was recently laid off and it has been very hard, especially with Christmas coming up. I can't imagine how difficult it is for my parents to know they can't get us everything for Christmas. As a child, you don't think of issues with money, but as an adult, your priorities with money change. "I experienced a different kind of fear as a staff officer and a senior commander (41). I believe this also relates to live. The age you are reveals how differently you will understand these predicaments.

Hard times change with age and wisdom. The experiences I have gone through in my life have made me a better person. Without the hard times I have gone through at the ages I have, I wouldn't be able to comprehend the hard times as easily and not break in half from the weight and responsibility as an adult with a family.

The silence is deafening. It seems like I am in a dark hole. I see a little light and down comes a rope, giving me ever so much hope. My parents have helped me every time I have fallen into that hole. My parents symbolize a rope braided together. When I am in a hole that rope comes down and helps pull me out. I realize now that maybe having a family that cares may also change how you deal with hard times. The rope of love and caring is my help and outlet in life. It helps to have a rope of your own when hard times come your way.

—Samantha Garcia, grade 11

Lesson 20:
Lyrics

Music plays a huge role in our lives, providing us with living soundtracks for our experiences. We associate songs with moments we've lived, moments packed with meaning and language.

   After students have a draft written, they can use song lyrics within their draft to bring the social context of their meanings to their readers.

Teaching It:

(Give students an index card.)
Take out your drafts. On the index card, write a word or phrase that tells what your piece is mostly about, or the main theme of your piece. *(Give them a couple of minutes, and then share out loud to stimulate ideas.)*

Now in your mind, scan through all the songs you've ever known and loved, and see if you can think of one that has to do with what you wrote on the card. Maybe it gives you the feeling of what's on your card.

When you think of one, don't sing it (or you'll jam someone else's thought waves), but write down some lines of lyrics, whatever comes to mind. We'll share in five minutes.

(After a couple of minutes, help those who are looking blank.)
Let me help you think of songs . . . think of songs on your favorite CDs . . . think of songs that were your favorites a few years ago . . . think of songs you loved when you were little . . . think of songs from movies . . . and if you don't get any ideas, don't worry. Maybe something will come to you when we share.

(After a few minutes, share themes and song connection ideas.)
If anyone didn't think of a song yet, maybe one will come to you after you sleep on it. Or maybe this idea didn't work for your piece. That's okay too.

Now, experiment with your essays, maybe by using some lines from a song in your draft.

Debriefing Questions:

How did you think of the songs you came up with?

Did anyone think of songs that just didn't fit? Like what?

What could you do with the lyrics now that you have some?

In what way could you use those in your piece? *(Discuss using them as frames or ribbons.)*

Another Debriefing Idea:

Ask students to write "how I did it" about how they made the choices they made.

Example:

My original brainstorming and drafts were filled with fake ideas that I created around a theme from the paper. After spending a great weekend with my friends, I was suddenly able to make dozens of connections based on friendships in the book!

The title "Lean on Me" came after I heard someone humming the tune to the song. I think by coming up with my own theme, I was able to make a more genuine connection. Plus, it was far easier for me to write about what I knew and then look for support, rather than finding a few support quotes and trying to tie in a connection.

—Katelyn Torok, grade 10

Student Samples:

Samples Using Lead Lyrics:

"Following the leader, the leader, the leader, we're following the leader, wherever he may go." That's what the British boys on the island [in Lord of the Flies] should have been singing instead of singing "kill the pig, slit his throat, spill its blood, smash its head" (Golding 69).

—Christina Meister, grade 10

Sample Using Woven Lyrics:

There's Nothing Better than Being a Kid

Baby Beluga
In the deep blue sea
It swims so wide
And it swims so free.
When do we really stop being a kid?
I believe there is nothing better than being a kid. You have no worries. You could always be yourself, not a care in the world but to have fun and get down and dirty.
Baby Beluga
In the deep blue sea
The boys from A Separate Peace would agree. Gene and Finny spend many afternoons climbing the tree, enjoying that be-yourself, not-a-care-in-the-world feeling, as they jump off into the water.
It swims so wide
And it swims so free.
Gene and Finny don't stop at the water's edge, though. Their freedom leads them to invent a new sport, "Blitzball," and they have no worries more boys join in. Finny invents the rules, and they play all summer.
I think I could relate to this, because I feel like I'm a kid all the time. I love to go to water parks. I sometimes wish I were still a kid so that I would have no worry and sleep and play all day. When I do something bad, I want to be a kid again so that my parents won't be so harsh on me, or give me bad punishment.
Baby Beluga
In the deep blue sea
It swims so wide
And it swims so free.
—Yanett Rodriguez, grade 10

Knowing Something in Your Heart

Lesson 21:
One Object

Inanimate objects can be powerful framing tools, evoking reflection and emotional reactions in the reader. They can signal flashbacks or foreshadowing in a narrative. Once a student has drafted an essay, this exercise can provide a sense of completeness, polish, and perspective.

Teaching It:

Do you remember the movie *Forrest Gump*? Do you remember the first thing you saw, before you even saw Forrest? *(Let them answer.)* That's right, a white feather. Do you remember the ending of the movie? Same thing, right? And the white feather also appeared during the middle of the movie somewhere, didn't it?

Look at your draft. See if you can think of one inanimate object that you could use to focus on at the beginning, before your piece kicks in, the same way as the white feather. You'll have to show it to us with words, instead of as part of a video. See if you can do the same thing. It might be an object you mentioned in the middle somewhere.

Think about it for a few minutes, and jot down some possible images you might use. *(Give them a couple of minutes, and then share ideas.)*
Give it a shot. Try writing up the image at the beginning, and again at the end. Let's just see what happens.
(Afterward, try reading some of the pieces with the new "frame." Discuss the effect.)

Debriefing Questions:

1. Who had an easy time thinking of an image? Can you tell us how it worked for you?

2. Who had a difficult time but thought of one?

3. How did the image change the feeling of the piece? Why did it?

Student Samples:

Cash drawer
Blue FFA jacket
Camera
Happy B-day in Spanish
Locket with a message
Eagle
Moving boxes
College diploma

Sample Essay Using an Object as a Frame

It's a tie game, 2–2, with 37 seconds left in the game. That's just enough time to make a goal. If only the puck would glide his way. Here it comes. He's been waiting for this opportunity ever since he got his new hockey stick. The puck glides effortlessly as his stick carries it down the rink. He can hear his coach screaming from the bench, "Go for it Terry. We need this goal. Shoot it!" Without even thinking about it he smacks his new stick against the puck. Crack! Suddenly the buzzard hollers its enormous cry. The game is over. Terry has made the winning goal, but this could be the end.

My dad has always been the strong willed type. The one who never lets you see him cry. He has also always had this energetic vibe that could be felt from miles away. He was ready and willing to do anything that required you to sign a Safety and Liability Form before allowing you to participate. If there is just one word to describe my dad, it would be sports. Ever since he was a little boy, he has been a sports fanatic. God help you if you change the channel when he's watching a hockey game, especially if it's the Flyers, so it's no wonder no one ever expected this to happen to him.

I was sitting outside with my boyfriend admiring his new Explorer. It had been a wonderful day. My dad was out of town, and although I missed him I was glad to get a break from the sports talk for a few days. I was laughing and having the time of my life as I blasted the music out of the Explorer's sound system. It was almost time for diner, which is around the time Dad would call to say hi. My mom walked outside. "Jessica, your dad is on the phone. (pause) Hurry up. He's calling long distance." I could tell something was wrong by the crackle in her voice. I honestly thought that my dad had some more work to do and was just calling to tell me that he would be staying in California a few more days. I told my boyfriend that I'd be right back. As soon as I walked inside and saw my mom crying, I knew I was not going to like what I was about to hear. I had been told a few days prior to this day that my dad had gone to the doctor for some testing, but no one had told me what for. They didn't want me to worry about it if it turned out to be a false alarm. Unfortunately, it wasn't a false alarm. Everyone gathered around the speakerphone.

"Hey guys. How was everyone's day today?" I had heard the same crackle in my mom's voice just moments before.

"Fine," we all answered.

My dad continued, "I'm really sorry that I have to tell you this over the phone, but you know that test I had done before I left? (pause) Well I have cancer. I'm sorry."

I couldn't believe it. I felt like my insides were going to burst into a ball of flames. At that moment a million thoughts were racing through my mind like a race car at the Indy 500.

"Are you going to die?" was all I could manage to say. I felt one single tear trickle down my face as the heat stung my cheek. I couldn't even conceive the thought that I might lose my dad.

He replied, "It's a type of cancer called prostate cancer. They caught it while it was in its early stages, so there's a good chance that I'll be fine. I'm just going to need some treatment. Hopefully there's nothing to worry about."

"Nothing to worry about!" I just stormed up to my room in a rage of fury. It really bothered me that he seemed to not be bothered by this whole thing. I was already going out of my mind. I realize now that that was his way of dealing with the thought of having cancer.

It was hard to sit there everyday and watch the man I once thought was so strong cry because the pain was so intense. I was not the first one moved by this experience and I probably won't be the last. It's hard for anyone to deal with. I can't even imagine how he felt knowing he would never be the same.

There it is. Just sitting in the corner of the garage. It hasn't been used in months. It has its battle scars and bruises. It has been the tool of victory for so many games. It has seen many tears shed and many cheers cried, so many players and coaches, yet it remains his most loyal friend. The hockey stick he got as a child remains dormant. There it lies in its never-ending sea of cobwebs and dust just waiting for that little boy to come out and play with it once more. But that little boy won't be coming out to play any more. That little boy has grown older. He is very weak now. It never thought it would see a grown man cry. I guess it was wrong.

—Jessica, grade 12

Lesson 22:
Dialogue

There can be no doubt that people listen to other people. In The Dialogic Imagination Mikhail Bakhtin wrote, "In the everyday speech of any person living in society, no less than half (on the average) of all the words uttered by him will be someone else's words" (339). And when we ask students to write some "academic," formal, uniform, non-human-sounding page full of words, we're asking them to discard our most natural tendency toward discourse: human conversation. So one way to tinker with the design of an essay is to experiment with dialogue.

Of course we teach students to write dialogue when they write narratives. But what about when they're writing expository or analytical pieces, like literary analyses? What could dialogue do for an analytical literary essay?

Literature is full of themes: disappointments in love, betrayal among friends, celebration of hard-won achievement, hope, legacies, change. We recognize themes because we have lived them. Dialogue from our lives can be a valid and effective link between an abstract thought and our actual realities. So using "life dialogue" as thick description is especially interesting and potentially powerful.

Teaching It:

(Give students an index card.)

Take out your drafts. On the index card, write a word or phrase that tells what your piece is mostly about, or the main theme of your piece. *(Give them a couple of minutes, and then share out loud to stimulate ideas.)*

You chose that main theme because you understand some things about it. You understand some things about it because it's been a part of your life, around you. Think about conversations you have heard where you have experienced that theme. Maybe they've been in the cafeteria; maybe they've been outside; maybe they've been in other settings. When one comes to mind, jot down a short conversation where that theme is evident, a conversation between two people, about three to five interchanges.

(Give students a few minutes, then share.)

Now, see what happens if you put snippets of that conversation in your paper. You might try using it in the beginning, or the end, or both, or throughout. You can repeat parts if you'd like, or add new parts. Just see what happens.

Debriefing Questions:

1. Did hearing other people's dialogues help you think of some?

2. Did the dialogue add to the piece of writing? How?

Student Samples:

It's the second day of school and I'm beginning to meet new people. I'm in my third period math and I notice a girl behind me crying.

Anna (me): Hi. I noticed you're crying and look rather lonely. Is there something I can help you with? What's your name?

Megan: My name is Megan and I am just going through a hard time with my parents. They've been married for sixteen years and have recently got a divorce.

Anna: I know who you feel since my parents divorced a while back. It's been hard telling people how I'm living two different lives, since my parents won't stop arguing. So I realize how hard it is for you.

Megan: Yes, my dad has just moved into his new apartment not far away from my mom. It makes me wonder if they ever thought how it would affect my life.

Anna: Before my parents split, they both told me that they still loved me, but they didn't love each other any more. They never could agree on anything.

Megan: That sounds bad. But how do you feel about writing that your parents are divorced on school records and telling your friends two different numbers which house you're at every weekend.

Anna: Yes at first it was miserable and I always tried to get them back together, but I got over it. All the arguing and fighting taught me a lesson -- never marry someone I won't always love.

(Five minutes left of class)

Anna: Well, there is not much time left in class, but what do you have next period?
Megan: Lunch.
Anna: Hey, so do I! Do you want to sit with me at lunch?
Megan: Sure.

(Bell rings to let third period out.)

Megan: It's nice to know that I'm not the only person whose parents are divorced. I hate dealing with all the problems they dumped on me, now I have someone to talk to about it.

–Sarah A Hogan, grade 10

Sample Woven Essay, Using Dialogue Expanded into a Woven Plot:

Brutality
(The Beast that Lurks Within)

"John is soooooooooo cute, but Josh is way funny! I can't believe they both like me. I just can't decide which one I like. Look at them arguing. They're probably just talking about me! Isn't it great? Oh my gosh! Josh just punched John."
"Fight!!!!"

Have you ever witnessed a violent or cruel act? Well, violence and cruelty are all around us in the world. They are even in literature. Mary Shelley and William Golding portray these themes in their novels, *Frankenstein* and *Lord of the Flies*. Even though they both show cruel and violent things, Frankenstein involves these themes more blatantly by numerous killings. Why do people do these things? This question remains unanswered for the time being.

In Lord of the Flies, William Golding displays some acts of violence and cruelty. For example, the boys get excited at almost killing a pig and they almost kill Robert. "Ralph carried away by a sudden thick, excitement, grabbed Eric's spear and jabbed at Robert with it. 'Kill him! Kill him!'" (114). Robert did not die, but the boys were very violent with him. They grabbed at him, the bit, and they even scratched at him.

Even though Robert gets away from the violence safely, Simon and Piggy do not. Simon and Piggy both die in this book over the spiteful actions of the other boys. When Simon is killed he is not just shot, but he is beat to death. "Kill the beast! Cut his throat! Spill his blood! Do him in!'... At once the crowd surged after it...lept onto the beast, screamed, struck bit, tore" (153). Simon dies only because the boys get caught up in all the excitement. Why did the boys turn to hostility? I'm sure the stress of the island was getting to them, but that's no excuse.

Aggression is also shown against Ralph when he refuses to join Jack and his "followers." Jack violently attacked Ralph. "Viciously, with full intention, he hurled his spear at Ralph. The point tore the skin and flesh over Ralph's ribs, then sheared off and fell in the water" (181). Jack was just actin gout of shear brutality. Many of the boys in this novel showed the same type of malice. Even Ralph, who was thought very highly of turned violent on his own friends.

"John and Josh fighting? But they're best friends. What have I done!"

Just as in *Lord of the Flies*, violence and cruelty are also present in Mary Shelley's *Frankenstein*. In this novel the Monster kills many people, including the main character. What makes it so cruel is that he doesn't kill instantly it is a slow and drawn out death. These killings leave horrifying pictures in the other characters' minds. Pictures that follow them wherever they go. This viciousness is shown in the aftermath of one of the monster's killings. "Her pale and distorted features half covered by her hair... her bloodless arms and relaxed form flung by the murderer..." (183). Frankenstein killed this girl with his bare hands. He violently beat her out of sheer cruelty and hatred.

Violence is also shown when the monster beat one of the cottagers. The cottagers had been very mean to him after they found out he had been watching them when in fact he was only trying to learn from them. "In a transport of fury, he dashed me to the ground and struck me violently with a stick" (123). The monster was very angry with the cottagers and he lashed out his anger on them by beating them. Even though the cottagers were mean to him it gave him no reason to return the unwanted favor. People do this often in society when they feel threatened.

"Jenny, come with me to see if we can stop them. I wish they didn't like me. I didn't want any of this to happen. I didn't mean for anybody to get hurt. If only I had told them. I didn't like either one of them."

Further more, cruelty can also be shown without words or violent actions. The silence of Dr. Frankenstein is an illustration of cruelty. He was too quiet through out the novel. He could have warned people about the monster he had created, but he didn't tell anybody so a lot of innocent people die.

"Josh, Josh it's me, Jeannine, please stop all this." John threw Josh to the floor. The sound of his head hitting the concrete echoed throughout the courtyard. Everyone stopped talking. It was silent except for the leaves sweeping across the blacktop.

Mr. Jay showed up soon to help. The sound of an ambulance coming up the street was heard. All the administrators come running towards bloody scene. "Move away from the boys!" "Back up!" "Give us some room!" "Who started this!" "Is he going to be okay?"

In contrast to *Lord of the Flies*, *Frankenstein* shows violence and cruelty more blatantly. In this novel many people are killed by these actions, while in *Lord of the Flies*, people are killed, but not as many as in *Frankenstein*. I feel that the killings show a different perspective of violence and curelty, than say a harsh beating because they actually involve a person being taken out of the world instead of just being injured.

Josh lay there still on the concrete. John bruised and cut with a confused look on his face, obviously ashamed of his actions. I could only wait and watch, hoping that Josh would be okay. Why did all this happen? How come people argue over things so small and simple?

I have come to the conclusion that violence and cruelty are everywhere and at first glance it seems there is nothing a person could do to stop it. But if you look harder, read between the lines, you grasp that most actions of violence are brought on by another's actions. Whether you realize it or not everything you do has an effect. The effect may be good or bad. This is what seems to cause violent or cruel things. The monster in *Frankenstein* was not violent until he was treated with disrespect. The boys from *Lord of the Flies* were not cruel until the actions of Jack led them to be. The beast within them was let out. Mary Shelly and William Golding try to bring these themes out in their novels to show people what effect their actions can have on other people. To try and teach a lesson to those of us who don't pay attention to what we do everyday. So be careful what you say and do because you never know when it will come back to you.

Works Cited

Golding, William. *Lord of The Flies*. New York: Berkley Publishing Group, 1954.
Shelly, Mary. *Frankenstein*. London, England: Pennyroyal Press. 1984.

—Jeannine Freeman, grade 11

Lesson 23:
Historical (or Other) Text

Familiar words from our culture stir up powerful reactions in us. As writers, we are more than a single, linear line of words on a page. The words that come out of our pens are a result of everything we are as people: our immediate circles of family and friends; people from our pasts; people we don't even know who have contributed text in our cultures.

Sometimes the familiar words of sacred or historical documents, inserted into our writing as snippets or allusions, can evoke powerful reactions in readers. They can also serve as text to interweave throughout text, with surprising results. Experimenting with them gives students another tool for their increasing arsenal of devices.

Teaching It:

(Give students an index card.)
There's text all around us. Words we hear other people say, words in our lives, those are all text.
Let's make a list of text you would recognize from our culture. From history. Who can think of one example of text, words, that every American would recognize? *(List all contributions, like the Pledge of Allegiance, the words of the Constitution or the Declaration of Independence, the words you hear in a newscast, poems you remember, words of famous speeches.)*

Take out your drafts. On the index card, write a word or phrase that tells what your piece is mostly about, or the main theme of your piece. *(Give them a couple of minutes, and then share out loud to stimulate ideas. Examples: loyalty, grief over losing someone.)*

See if you can think of a document or speech that is about that theme. Now under the theme, jot down the words if you know them, or the idea of what kind of text might be related. If you can't think of any, just wait. You'll get ideas later.

(Give them a few minutes, and then share.)

Now try placing snippets of that text throughout your draft, and let's just see what happens.
(Show student samples below, if needed.)

Debriefing Questions:

1. What happened when you placed the text into your draft?

2. Where are some good sources of texts?

3. How do you manage if you don't know the words?

Spin-offs:

Try text that contrasts with the theme in your piece, for ironic effect. (Listen to Simon and Garfunkel's "7 O'Clock News/Silent Night.")

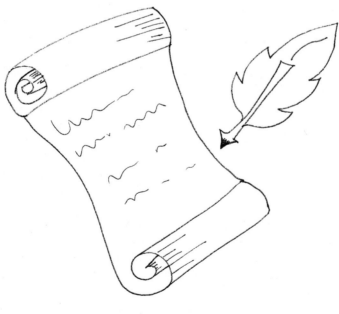

Hannah Wells

Student Samples:

Sample Essays with Woven Sacred or Historical Text
Trials and Tribulations

Death must be easy, because life is hard! Without a life full of hardship, we as humans beings (especially in America) wouldn't realize or understand how great life is. We tend to take things for granted until they are gone, and once they are gone, we don't know how to handle the hardship of it.

Thy kingdom come
Thy will be done
Here on Earth
As it is in Heaven

Some people think that a hardship can completely destroy a person's mind, body, and soul. At a very young age I learned that a hardship could change an entire person and their outlook on life.

When I was seven, my mom's mother died. Ever since my mom has never been the same and I miss who she use to be. I don't enjoy hearing my mom comparing herself to my grandmother. I love her for being my mom, not for being her mom. Till this day I can promise you that my mom cries for my grandmother at least twice a day.

Thy kingdom come

In the town of Salem, this proved to be true. The town and its people were practically destroyed due to the "wild things" (177) that Abigail and the girls said. The girls also showed that "envy is a deadly sin" (224) that could tear any friendship apart when lies are involved.

Thy will be done

However some people think that a hardship can make one stronger. My grandmother's death doesn't seem affect me. My grandmother died two months after being diagnosed with colon cancer. In the two months it seemed like grandmother's immune system ate her alive. I just feel that it would be selfish of me to want her knowing how much pains she was in.

Here on Earth

John and Goody Proctor's marriage was on the rocks and it seemed like it wasn't going to get any better. Due to John committing adultery, their relationship got to the point of Elizabeth being able to 'freeze beer" (194) with her attitude towards John. But due to the town ignorance, their relationship was almost once again, and Elizabeth realized it. "He has his goodness and God forbid I take it from him" (240).

As it is in Heaven

I, on the other hand, think that people view a crisis differently due to the various personalities and their different experiences. I do feel that when older and mature my view on this subject might be completely different.

Thy Kingdom come
They will be done
Here on Earth
As it is in Heaven

—Lauren C. Potts, grade 11

I Pledge Allegiance

I pledge allegiance to the flag and to the Republic for which it stands: one nation, indivisible, with liberty and justice for all.

Being loyal can save or destroy a human's soul. It can bring a family together or destroy a friendship. The big question is can loyalty be the biggest part of human characteristics?

Odysseus in "The Odyssey" is very loyal to his men. He will do anything to save as many of them as he can, even at the cost of his own life and other's lives. It says in the book, "against Eurylochus' advice, however, Odysseus rushes to save his men from the enchantress" (920). His loyalty saved many lives.

I pledge allegiance...

The sniper in "The Sniper" was loyal to the Republicans. He fought in a deadly war. It states in the book, "he must kill the enemy" (165). It shows that he is truly loyal to the Republicans at all cost.

...to the flag and to the Republic for which it stands:

The sniper may have been too loyal. He killed because he was loyal, "The eyes of a man who is used to looking at death" (164). In which doing, he ended up killing his brother.

Being loyal can also make you do something you don't like. Say you're loyal to a friend and they tell you a secret that could be fatal. What would you do? Or you could be so loyal to someone you depend on them, and what would happen if they weren't there for you?

In "The Scarlet Ibis" Doodle is so dependent on his brother, the narrator, it turns to be fatal, "I began to weep, and the tear-blurred vision in red before me look very familiar" (604). It became the ultimate sacrifice for the narrator.

But was he just pretending to be loyal? "He was a burden in many ways" (596). It shows that the narrator was burdened by Doodle and wasn't truly loyal till later in the story. As you can see, pain and joy can come from being loyal, but sometimes we wonder if the joy is worth the pain. Some seem to believe so. I believe in certain cases it's worth it. Loyalty can be like a faithful dog that is always there for you, or maybe a lover who will stand by your side forever. Loyalty has to be one of the most important qualities of a human being because sometimes it can make the difference between life or death.

...one nation, indivisible, with liberty and justice for all.

—Jessica Lipsett, grade 9

4

Crafting The Essay for a Reader's Ears

Drafting It: Tips

Drafting the essay should be a walk in the park now. Students will have found (or devised) a truism or other message they can talk about; they will have chosen (or devised) a text structure; they will have scratched around for some thick description possibilities. At this point, the writer should be able to pretend she's telling someone the whole thing, and just write down what she would say.

But sometimes students summarize so much and elaborate so little, the following strategies can bring relief, whether in the drafting stage or as revision.

Snapshots. Imagine a photo of something you're describing, and freeze the frame in your head, giving yourself time to describe all the details you would see in a snapshot. (For more about this technique, see Barry Lane's *After THE END*.)

Thoughtshots. Insert the mental dialogue you'd be having at a given moment. Put in everything that would have been going through the character's head at that moment. (For more information about thoughtshots, see Barry Lane's *After THE END*.)

Depth charging. Isolate a potentially vague or meaningful word or phrase that you'd like to tell more about, and write a sentence explaining that word. Then choose a word or phrase in the new sentence, and write a sentence explaining that. Then go on with what you were saying. (For more information about depth charging, see Joyce Armstrong Carroll's *Dr. JAC's Guide to Writing with Depth*.)

Brushstrokes. Imagine that your words are paint, and that you're painting an image for your reader. Use grammatical constructions like participial phrases, absolutes, adjectives out of order, and strong verbs to add visual brushstrokes to your image. (For more information about brushstrokes, see Harry Noden's *Image Grammar*.)

Three questions. Imagine your reader listening and wanting to know more about what you're saying. Imagine what three questions he'd ask as you tell your story, and write the answers into your words to answer those questions ahead of time. (For more information about the three questions technique, see Barry Lane's *After THE END*.)

In addition to these, the following lessons provide "strategic hits" on several problem areas and can change the ways in which writers approach their drafts.

Lesson 24:
Knowing Something

You can know something in your head, and you can know something in your heart. There's a huge difference, a difference that readers can tell. It's obvious when you've read something "heartfelt." But what do writers do to show they know something in their heart? This exercise will raise their awareness of what specific things writers do to create this effect on readers.

Just as in other craft-borrowing exercises, writers 1) examine an effective piece of writing; 2) analyze the construction; and 3) imitate it. In this particular model, the essay suggests a narrative movement from "knowing something in your head" to "knowing something in your heart."

Teaching It:

What's the most important thing in your life? (Family, friends.)

On an index card, list the five most important things in your life, besides family and friends. *(Pause.)*

Now, for each one of those, write a sentence that shows one thing you truly know about that thing. *(Pause.)*

Now, put these aside. We're going to read an essay written by a student. In it, there's something brilliant that I want you to see. *(Read the sample essay by Cassandra Lopez.)*

In this essay, Cassandra talked about how memories of bad times stick with you. Did she know this in her head or her heart? It was pretty clear that this student knew what she was talking about, in her heart. But how did you get that impression? Which parts made you think that?

(Identify the parts, and highlight them.)

Now choose one of your statements. In the next twenty minutes, write about it. Try to show in your writing that you know with your heart, and not just with your head. *(Write, share, and debrief.)*

Debriefing Questions:

1. How did you structure it? ("Oh look . . . you began with an anecdote. Oh look . . . yours is a narrative of the chronology . . .")

2. What about this structure worked for you?

3. Why does narrative writing have clearer links than expository writing?

Student Sample

Have you ever tried thinking as far back as you can remember? Well I'm sitting here trying to remember as far back as I can, but the only problem is that when I try thinking about my past I can only remember the bad things. The furthest thing I can remember is one day I was sitting down trying to finish eating dinner which was spaghetti and green beans. I hate green beans. I was about 5 or 6, and I was too full, but my father didn't care about that and ordered me to finish eating or I would be put in time-out.

"But Papa I don't want anymore!" I cried.

My mom heard me and came from the kitchen to help me. Then out of nowhere, the doorbell rings. My father got up from the couch and answered the door.

It was a mid-age man with glasses and a short blond lady, nobody I had seen before. They were standing there with a friendly smile and looking completely harmless. But then the man spoke the words I will never forget...

"Hello, we're here for the dog."

I dropped my fork and I couldn't breathe. I kept repeating what they said over and over in my head. What did he mean ... here for the dog? My dog—not theirs, I thought. I took a long gasping breath.

"Mommy!" I whispered.

"It's O.K." my mom comforted.

"No!" I cried.

"Don't cry," my mom said sternly.

What do you mean, "don't cry"? I couldn't help but to cry. I ran outside and held MY Dog, MY Pepe. No they couldn't take him from me, it was like he was my only friend, my only companion, my buddy, he was there thick and thin, and now my parents were giving him away, trashing him like an old pillow that's been there for you comforting you when you need it, one that can just sit there and listen to you and says all the right things without saying a word. That's what Pepe was to me, and now he was going to be gone forever.

For classroom duplication only. Enlarge at 121% for 81/2 x 11 sheet

Reviving The Essay © 2005 Discover Writing Press • www.discoverwriting.com   125

As I watched my father and this man I now considered "The Enemy" talk, I was thinking to myself why are they doing this to me? Giving away my dog, my only friend? Why? It was because we were moving, and we were moving because my father is in the military, which explains his harshness towards my feelings of discomfort. We were moving far, far away from my friends, my school, my house, and now my dog.

My father and The Enemy came outside; my father gave me a hard look as to say 'get your butt inside' but I didn't move a muscle. So he grabbed me by the arm, dragged me to the table, and yet again ordered me to finish eating. The tears flowed down my face. I looked down at my plate and I despised everything on it, all 23 green beans and 2 meatballs; I hated my parents; I hated the man and his short wife; and I hated the fact we were moving. I sat there and watched them put the leash on my dog and drag my dog away. What a memory huh?

It seems to me that good memories may stay with you, but the bad memories are easier to remember.

—Cassandra M. Lopez, grade 9

For classroom duplication only. Enlarge at 121% for 81/2 x 11 sheet

126   **Reviving The Essay** © 2005 Discover Writing Press • www.discoverwriting.com

The Winds of November

It was a bitterly cold day of an even colder month. It was on a Tuesday in November, the day she was diagnosed. My brother and I drove home from school both yet unaware of the events to come. From what I remember it was the wind that made it cold, but my recollections of that day still have trouble playing back in my mind. I gazed out the car window on the ride home; and even with the stereo blaring I could think just fine. I stared at fallen leaves soaring in the November wind, wondering if one day I could be like them. If I could be free, not held down by anything or anyone. My father was sitting on the front porch with a look on his face I had not seen in a long time. When my brother and I stepped up to the front porch he told us the news. "Your mother went to the doctor today and … the cancer has returned … except this time it's terminal." My brother almost fell to the ground out of remorse and shock. My mother was in bed upstairs and the walk to her room was the longest of my life. Every blistering step brought me closer to painful reality that in less than two months my mother would be gone. I stepped slowly into the room with a blank stare on my face, and through all her pain she smiled at me. At this I felt relieved for this showed me that she was not afraid. We never addressed the illness directly and never mentioned the creeping future.

For two months I lied by her side, playing guitar and singing songs I had written for her, never had I seen my mom happier than those last months. Towards the end her energy began to fade along with her smile and the light in her eyes. The pain was too much to bear for her; her time was approaching. I lie at her side the morning of Tuesday December 24 and what she said next I shall never forget. She said, "Don't worry. I'm not afraid to die. I find it peaceful and lovely sort of. I will finally be free of all the pain, like a leaf blowing in the open wind. The only pain I'll be left with is the pain of never seeing you or your brother again. I want you to always enjoy life and live every day to the fullest because you will never know when life will throw you a curve ball and a routine doctor's visit tells you that you have two months to live. You need to always be free and never let anyone hold you down or hold you back. I love you both." At this, my mother let out her last breaths and a small tear fell from her eye.

She was buried on Dec 26, my parents anniversary. Both my brother and I took her final words to heart. My brother is in his third year at United States Military Academy at West Point, and is soon to be married. I never have let anyone or anything hold me down from my dreams. I am the free leaf blowing in the winds of November soaring above it all.
—Andrew Reynosa, grade 10

Lesson 25:
Ba-da-bing! A Sentence-Imitating Exercise

When a reader "gets lost" in the writing, it almost feels like they've "slipped into the skin" of the writer. This is a goal of good writing, to engage the reader so much that they can imagine living the experience they're reading about. So how do writers do this? As C. S. Lewis said, "Don't say it was 'delightful'; make us say 'delightful' when we've read the description. You see, all those words (horrifying, wonderful, hideous, exquisite) are only like saying to your readers 'Please will you do my job for me.'"

So which grammatical constructions create this effect for a reader? The "ba-da-bing" sentence is one such construction. It consists of three parts: where the speaker was physically, what they saw, and what they thought. This construction works, because sometimes writers need help making their moments translate to the same kinds of moments for their readers. This sentence-imitating exercise is easy for all ages and can produce rich results for the reader.

Teaching It:

(Draw three icons—foot, eye, thought bubble—on a chalkboard or transparency.)
Find an important moment in your memory piece, and I'll show you a trick. Write a sentence with these three parts:

Where your feet went ,

what you saw ,

and what you thought.

Here's an example: **When I went (point to the feet) into the kitchen, I saw (point to the eye) my mom at the stove, stirring a pot. Mmmm, I thought. Chili!**

Now you try one.

Debriefing Questions:

1. Was that difficult?

2. How many of these would you want in your piece?

3. Is there only one way to punctuate this?

Spin-offs:

1. Find a "moment" in your piece and underline the sentence. Write a ba-da-bing and tuck it in. Repeat two more times. Share.

2. Post ba-da-bings on sentence strips and compare sentence structure, tone.

3. Change the "eye" part to other senses.

4. Celebrate when students use more vivid verbs than "walked" and "saw" and "thought."

5. Write "Who Am I" sentences from literature and let students identify the speaker.

Student Samples:

I walked into the kitchen and saw my mother holding a skateboard, and I thought, "Hey! Is that for me?"   —Torrey, grade 2

When I was sitting quietly in the room I saw him walk in and thought, "Oh, please! Don't let it be me! Please, oh please!"   —Nicolle, grade 4

When I walked out of the car and I saw my grandpa for the last time, I thought, "Will he still be in my heart?"   —Nigel, grade 6

When I drove into Plainview and I saw the Wal-Mart, I thought, "Oh, everything will be okay." —Israel, grade 6

When I stepped out onto the stage, I couldn't see the audience because the lights were in my eyes. What was I so afraid of? I thought. This is fun. —Matilde Bernabei, grade 6

I walked into the classroom. I saw the most beautiful girl. I thought that girl will change my life. —Jonathan Farias, grade 7

Ba-da-bing Samples by Beginning ESOL High School Students

Note: ESOL teacher Jann Fractor writes: "The students were writing a language experience story together. Their story centered on the habitat of animals in the San Antonio Zoo. They decided to 'visit' the fictional director and suggest a more natural habitat. At that point I walked them through Ba-da-bing. It worked! These students have been in the United States five months! These are uncorrected samples."

I walk into the office. I see Mr. Jones setting at his desk talking on the phone. I think that I should wait to talk. —Ana, grade 9

As I walk in to the office I see it a little careless, many papers some on the table, on the floor, also have bookseller [file cabinet] open. I see the Director setting playing in the computer.
I think is no a good Director because the zoo need more attencion. —Elvia, grade 9

As I walk into the office I see differents kinds of animals posters and in to the one of the sides one bookcase with many books about animals, nutrition, medicine and is smell like roses and fruits. And in the front I see the desk with one computer and in here I see the cameras in the zoo, and in the other side I see the director of the zoo, is a woman, taller, brownhear [brown hair], glasses, honey eyes, with pants and boots, her shirt is like cowgirl but she look like workwomen and she was standing and look one book about medicine because she was worry about animals, what she can do for the animals? Why? I think the director is a very good because she was worry for the animals and that will be ok....
—Rocio, grade 9

Sample "Who Am I" Ba-da-bing Sentences from Fairy Tales

In a deep sadness I descended the stairs, lifted my head to catch sight of a true beauty in my own mansion, and thought, she could make all my sadness go away. —Will B., grade 9

When I strolled over the hill and glimpsed the straw house by the creek, my stomach growled. This will be easy to blow down! —Tyler, grade 9

As I dragged myself to the top of the beanstalk, I peeked over the top of the beanstalk and gazed upon a huge castle and wondered who lived in there. —Anthony, grade 9

Sample "Who Am I" Ba-da-bings from *To Kill a Mockingbird*

As I waltzed over to my window, I glanced at a kid rolling into my fence with a tire. How funny! —Luke, grade 9

I was walking down the street with Scout, and I saw Tim Johnson walking funny, and I thought something was wrong and that we should go home and tell Calpurnia. —Tyrell, grade 9

When I walked towards Tim Johnson, I saw him lying there in a puddle of blood and thought, "Dude. I have to clean that up." —Brandon M., grade 9

The following chart demonstrates teachable areas through the varied sentence formations in these sentences.

Sample Ba-da-bing Free-Choice Reading Response, by Alyssa M., grade 9

Variations	Ba	Da	Bing	Teachable
Three sentences (simple)	I walked up on the stage.	I saw a person handing me a paper rolled up with a red ribbon.	I thought, "I made it."	Point of view: student speaks as narrator; play with 3rd person switch.
Two sentences (complex and simple)	When I walked up on the stage,	I saw a person handing me a paper rolled up with a red ribbon.	I realized that I had made it.	Direct and indirect thoughts can be punctuated differently.
One sentence (compound-complex)	When I walked up on the stage,	I saw a person handing me a paper rolled up with a red ribbon.	and I thought, "I made it."	Subordinating the first clause creates smoothness; play with subordinating the second clause instead.
Two sentences (complex and simple)	When I walked up on the stage,	I saw a person handing me a paper rolled up with a red ribbon.	I had made it.	Implying "I thought" shows syntactic maturity

For classroom duplication only. Enlarge at 121% for 81/2 x 11 sheet

Reviving The Essay © 2005 Discover Writing Press • www.discoverwriting.com   **131**

Lesson 26:
Look What You Wrote! (Finding Well-Done Mechanics, Rhetorical Devices, and Beauty)

This activity gets students thinking of themselves as writers.

When you, the teacher, hold up a sentence written by one of your students and say, "Look at the genius right here…" several things happen. First, students pay real attention, because one of them wrote it. Second, students feel heard and appreciated. Third, the writer of the sentences feels the flush of fame that stays with him or her forever. And finally, students actually learn and remember the literary or rhetorical device they find in the sentence. It doesn't matter whether the teacher calls it by its literary name (like a chiasmus) or by a new classroom nickname (like "that kind of sentence that Perry wrote" which becomes "the Perry trick"). The students' awareness of the device is changed, and they may add it to their bag of rhetorical tools. It takes virtually no classroom time.

Teachers often use daily language warm-ups, in which students focus on mistakes in a sentence or two from prepackaged sources. The same amount of classroom time could be used in a more meaningful and powerful way.

This activity focuses on positive grammatical and rhetorical constructions of sentences written by students in the classroom. Students may not think about the craft of how they say things the first time, but after you help them notice the devices they already use intuitively, they may consider using them intentionally.

Used routinely, this practice can cause students to make a shift in the way they read. As Frank Smith says in "Essays into Literacy":

> We find ourselves pausing while we read . . . not because of a spelling and certainly not for lack of understanding, but simply because we have just read something that is particularly well put, an interesting idea appropriately expressed. This time we have engaged not with a spelling or even with a convention of punctuation or grammar, but with a style, a tone, a register. We are learning vicariously, reading as if we ourselves might be doing the writing, so that the author's act in effect becomes our own. This, I think, is the secret of learning to write by reading—by reading like a writer. (103)

Teaching It:

(Prep: when you read student writing, copy powerfully written sentence samples onto transparencies.)

Let's look at a sentence written by one of you. *(Show one.)* This sentence is especially effective. Listen as I read it to you. *(Read aloud.)* I'm going to read it again, and this time, listen to what the writer did that helped make this sentence so strong. *(Read it again.)* What did you hear that makes this sentence powerful? *(Listen to each idea from students, agreeing and naming each skill.)*

Debriefing Questions:

1. When you look at your own writing, can you tell which sentences are the most powerful?

2. Did the author use this device (like parallelism, brevity, repetition, chiasmus) on purpose, or did it just come out that way?

Spin-offs:

1. Each time you and your students name a grammatical construction or rhetorical device, post it on a classroom poster.

2. Collect powerful sentences from literature you're reading in class, chosen most effectively by your students, to post, analyze, and imitate.

3. "Devolve" the powerful sentences to show students "the way an ordinary writer would say it," followed by the way the student wrote it. (See the template at the end of this lesson.)

Resources:

Joyce Armstrong Carroll's *Dr. JAC's Guide to Writing with Depth* is an amazing resource for writers, making rhetorical and literary devices accessible to writers of all levels.

In the appendix of her book *What You Know by Heart*, Katie Wood Ray offers a wonderful beginning list of constructions writers use, with samples.

Student Samples:

Sometimes I wonder, does every hero need his armor, or does every piece of armor need its hero.
—Perry Martinez, grade 9

Some people believe that ghosts are real and others think it's just a bunch of tall tales.
—John Cronin, grade 9

Boo Radley is somewhat like a ghost story: you don't really see him, but there are stories.
—Megan James, grade 9

If the world put labels on the people in it, then we would have no way of being special, unique or different.
—Alyssa Sanchez, grade 9

Our parents still listen to their parents.
—Daniel Bernal, grade 10

Some people may be lucky enough to have an idyllic childhood replete with summers with Mom and Dad in the country, fireflies in a jar, and noodle salad. The rest of us aren't so lucky.
—Pam John, Teacher

Even the city has us on lockdown. —Valerie Garcia, grade 10

To be betrayed by a friend is a lot worse than being betrayed by an enemy because a friend is the one you trust and to learn that the trust is fake hurts a lot more.
—Jennifer Cooper, grade 10

Emotional scars are worse than physical scars. —Vincent Aguilera, grade 10

I'm sure it has happened to many people and I know it hurts. —Melissa Morales, grade 10

Betrayal by a friend is like something that will always be remembered, but an attack by an enemy will be forgotten sooner or later. —Jorge Reyna, grade 10

An enemy doesn't know anything about you, but a friend knows everything about you.
—Blanca Mata, grade 10

Will this ever happen to me? —Roseann Renteria, grade 10

I think it's okay because it teaches us respect, manners, and responsibility, and even discipline. —David Rodriguez, grade 10

You don't realize how special children are until you have them and then nature takes over; like a mother bear protects her baby cubs, you would protect your children and fight for them with your very life if you have to. —Tracey Myers, Teacher

Spin-off Examples:

The way an ordinary writer would say it:
I wasn't a good player, and I got embarrassed, so my dad helped me.

The way YOU said it:
The very first time I played with a team called the Eagles. When someone passed me the ball, all I did was pass it back to that person. When I tried to shoot, it was an airball. I was so embarrassed everyone was laughing at me except my dad. After that day, my dad has been working with me.
Emily Segura, grade 7

The way an ordinary writer would say it:
When she talks to me, it makes me feel good.

The way YOU said it:
Sometimes when I'm not happy, she could just be calling to see how I'm doing, and just hearing her voice on the other end of the phone brings a big Kool-aid smile to my face.
—April N. Caudillo, grade 7

For classroom duplication only. Enlarge at 121% for 81/2 x 11 sheet

Reviving The Essay © 2005 Discover Writing Press • www.discoverwriting.com   **135**

Lesson 27:
Devolved Essays

Most sample papers shown to students are written by different writers. In other words, a high-scoring paper is written by one student, and a low-scoring paper is written by a different writer. This gives students the idea that there are different kinds of writers: good writers who write good papers, and poor writers who write poor papers. What happens next? Students mentally compare themselves to the writers of the papers and "cast themselves" into the writing that most resembles their work. That creates a bias in students' minds, a bias that is difficult to change. Teachers hear students say things like, "I don't write 3's; I write 4's." Or, "Yeah, right...those 1's? That's me."

This exercise undoes that self-stereotyping and demonstrates this: There are not kinds of students; there are kinds of papers. A devolved paper shows every stage of a paper: the same paper, beginning at the end with its effective state, and slowly demolished until it's not effective at all.

How does it work? Look at the sample papers that follow, devolved with a 4-point rubric. You'll find samples from grade 4, devolved by teachers in San Antonio, followed by a grade 7 piece devolved by middle school teacher Darla White.

The first paper is a high-scoring paper by a fourth grader. You'll notice some bold parts. These are the "best parts," or those parts that our team of readers just liked the most. Now look at the paper that follows, the 3. It's another version of the very same paper, with some of the bold parts removed or weakened to show how a lesser writer would have written them. There are still bold portions, because this paper is still very strong. The next paper, the 2, shows the paper in its next weakest state, and the final paper demonstrates how that paper would look as an ineffective version of itself, a lowly 1.

Students look at the four versions, reading them and deciding which parts would be the strong parts. Then they view the next versions. By the time they have finished sharing the language of the lowest paper, they understand something new about scores. Scores may have nothing to do with the creativity of the idea in the paper, or with the extraordinary experiences of the writer. They have nothing to do with what "kind of a writer" the writer is. They have everything to do with "what kind of a paper" the writer decides to produce—how well the writer gives an experience to the reader.

Rather than using these samples exclusively, you'll find this lesson is most effective if you take a high-scoring paper from your own campus and devolve it.

How do you go about "devolving" an essay? Locate a well-written piece and get the writer's permission to "mess with the paper." (They're usually delighted!) Highlight all the parts you think make the paper work well. Then remove just enough of them to bump the paper down to a lower-scoring paper. Continue this process until you have several versions of the same paper. You'll have to reword some sentences, make some specific parts more general, and make some in-depth parts skim the surface. The rubric that you're using will help give guidelines as you strip out the effective parts of it in increments similar to the sample. In other words, is a "2" characterized by gaps in logic? Then have some fun getting some gaps into that paper at the "2" stage. Make sure to leave the author's name only on the author's version.

Students will then be able to see the real differences in what works for a reader.

Teaching It:

Let's read a really effective paper together. *(Do, on the overhead.)* What were the best parts? What parts stand out to you as the most memorable? What parts do you remember first? *(Highlight all the best parts, as students volunteer them.)* What would happen to this paper if we took those parts out? How would it sound?

(Show them the next lowest stage of the devolved paper.) The paper would look like this. What about it is still effective? *(Transitions that are clear, points that are still strong.)* What would happen if we took out some of those transitional parts? And made the points a little more muddy, less clear, less strong? What if we weakened it up some more?

(Show them the next lowest stage of the devolved paper.) The paper would look like this. What about it is still effective? *(It still makes its point in a clear enough way.)* What if we pulled out some of the backup and made the point without much illustration at all?

(Show them the lowest stage of the devolved paper.) The paper would look like this.

Debriefing Questions:

1. In all four cases, do you think the writer had something to say? Then what made the difference?

2. Was it easy to see the best parts in the highest-scoring version?

3. Do all the versions have something good about them? What?

Spin-offs:

1. Devolve another paper in groups. Post copies of the versions of the paper in the room, in poster size.

2. Devolve individual sentences from essays or from literature.

3. Identify the writing devices (whether literary, like similes, or grammatical, like clauses, or rhetorical, like use of repetition) in the high paper (even for young children), list them on a wall chart, and practice them individually. Make personal lists of devices that students can use as tools, and keep them in student writing folders or journal glossaries.

* Elementary teacher Rebecca Shapiro keeps wall charts of Harry Noden–style "brush-strokes" from her students' pieces. Lifting all those parts out would be a simple devolving step.

Grade 4—Score Point 4

"Aww, Mom it's only 5:30!" I **complained as I slowly slithered out of bed like an exhausted snake.**

"Yes I know but it's going to take a long time to get to Dallas." she replied. **I yawned as I pulled on my red and black leotard, black warm-ups,** and **sparkly** tennis shoes. We were driving to Dallas for my level 5 state meet. I was very excited! I love gymnastics. I have been in for 6 years, **since I was a silly little 4 year old.** Now I am 9 and I am pretty good at it.

After I packed my **new "Sunburst" bag** with my grips, extra hair stuff and a snack, I jumped down the stairs and into the kitchen. **I could smell delicious cinnamon rolls and eggs cooking.** When I finished **eating a feast** of 4 cinnamon rolls and a pile of cheesy, ketchupy eggs, I **skipped** into the small bathroom to get a hairbrush and pony-tail holder. My mom pulled my hair into a perfect ponytail, stuck in 6 clips and sprayed it with hairspray. Finally we were ready to go. I put **my adorable Cocker Spaniel** puppy in the backyard and locked the door. Then I grabbed my bag, ran out the front door, and slipped into our Ford Escape **as fast as a baseball player would slide into home base.** The rest of my family jumped in and we were off!

The long drive was very boring **and time consuming**, but it was worth it. When we got there I saw bright, white lights, and **millions** of people everywhere. Soon every-one sat down though, so we could start competing. My team's first event was bars, and I was 3rd up. When it was my turn I did everything with a tight body. The judges gave me a 9.285! **It was amazing!** Next we had beam, and I was 1st. I did a great routine except when I wobbled on my leap. I only got a 9.275, **but I didn't care.** On floor I did one of my best routines and got a 9.5. That wasn't too bad. Last was vault, my worst event. I needed at least a 9.4 to get my best all-around a 38.00. On my turn I ran like a **ferocious German Shepherd** was chasing me, stayed tight and got a 9.4! I got 3rd place in Texas with a 38.00.

Wow! What a great day! **I got** 3rd place **and I got** three of my highest scores in the season, a 9.825 on bars, a 9.4 on vault and a 38.00 all-around. Now I get to be a level 6 gymnast. **That means lots of fun new skills!** I think that even though I had to wake up early, the day of my state meet was the best day I ever had!

Score point: 4. This smooth and unified piece is easy for a reader to visualize. The writer includes plenty of interpretive thought along with the action, so the reader understands the impact of the events. Dialogue and sentence variety add to its effectiveness.

For classroom duplication only. Enlarge at 121% for 81/2 x 11 sheet

Reviving The Essay © 2005 Discover Writing Press • www.discoverwriting.com   **139**

Grade 4—Score Point 3

"Aww, Mom it's only 5:30!" I slithered out of bed like an exhausted snake.
"Yes I know but it's going to take a long time to get to Dallas." she replied. I
yawned as I pulled on my **red and black leotard, black warm-ups, and tennis shoes.**
We were driving to Dallas for my level 5 state meet. **I was very excited! I love gym-**
nastics. I have been in for 5 years. Now I am 9 and I am pretty good at it.

After I packed my **new bag** with **my grips, extra hair stuff and a snack**, I jumped
down the stairs and into the kitchen. I could smell **delicious cinnamon rolls and eggs**
cooking. When I finished **4 cinnamon rolls and a pile of eggs, I skipped** into the
small bathroom to get a **hairbrush and ponytail holder.** My mom pulled my hair into a
perfect ponytail, **stuck in 6 clips and sprayed it with hairspray.** Finally we were ready
to go. **I put my cute puppy in the backyard and locked the door. Then I grabbed my**
bag, ran out the front door, and slipped into our Ford Escape. The rest of my family
jumped in and we were off!

The long drive was very boring, **but it was worth it.** When we got there I saw
bright, white lights, and lots of people everywhere. **Soon everyone sat down though,**
so we could start competing. My team's first **event** was bars, and I was 3rd up. When
it was my turn **I did everything with a tight body.** The judges gave me a 9.285! It was
cool! Next we had beam, and I was 1st. **I did a great routine except when I wobbled**
on my leap. I only got a 9.275. On floor I did one of my best routines and got a 9.5.
That wasn't too bad. Last was vault, my worst event. **I needed at least a 9.4 to get**
my best all-around a 38.00. On my turn I ran like a mean dog was chasing me,
stayed tight and got a 9.4! I got 3rd place in Texas with a 38.00.

What a great day! I got 3rd place and **I got three of my highest scores in the**
season, a 9.825 on bars, a 9.4 on vault and a 38.00 all-around. Now I get to be a
level 6 gymnast. **I think that even though I had to wake up early**, the day of my state
meet was the best day I ever had!

Score point: 3. The piece is unified and vivid enough to sustain a reader's interest. The
writer's use of conventions and figurative language is fluent and effective.

For classroom duplication only. Enlarge at 121% for 81/2 x 11 sheet

140   **Reviving The Essay** © 2005 Discover Writing Press • www.discoverwriting.com

Grade 4—Score Point 2

I woke up at 5:30. I got out of bed. "Yes, I know but it's going to take a long time to get to Dallas," my mom said. **I yawned as I got dressed.** We were driving to Dallas for my level 5 state meet. I have been in gymnastics for 5 years. Now I am 9 and am pretty good at it.

After I packed my bag with my stuff, I went into the kitchen. I could smell food cooking. When I finished eating, I went into the bathroom to do my hair. My mom put my hair into a ponytail. Finally we were ready to go. I put my puppy in the backyard and got into the car.

The long drive was very boring. **When we got there I saw lots of people.** The first thing I did was bars. I did good. I got a 9.825. It was cool. Second we did the beam, and I was first. I only got a 9.275. Third was floor and I got a 9.5. **Last was vault, my worst event.** On my turn I got a 9.4! I got 3rd place in Texas.

What a great day! I got 3rd place all-around. Now I get to move up a level. The day of my state meet was the best day I ever had.

Score point: 2. This piece generally conveys the events and why the day was important to the writer. There are a few gaps and some vagueness, but the piece does include enough idea development and progression from sentence to sentence and paragraph to paragraph to make it at least minimally effective.

For classroom duplication only. Enlarge at 121% for 81/2 x 11 sheet

Reviving The Essay © 2005 Discover Writing Press • www.discoverwriting.com 141

Grade 4—Score Point 1

I got out of bed we went to Dallas. **First I was** on the bars and got third. The girl before me had on a pretty purple leotard. **She did** not do so good I wish I hadn't had eggs for breakfast. **I did** a bunch of other **things** I was good and I got third in Texas and this is why I had the best day in my life

Score point: 1. This piece shows serious errors in sentence boundaries that interfere with its effectiveness. The ideas are so superficially developed that the reader does not get a sense of the voice of the writer.

For classroom duplication only. Enlarge at 121% for 81/2 x 11 sheet

142 **Reviving The Essay** © 2005 Discover Writing Press • www.discoverwriting.com

Grade 7—Score Point 4

Swoosh

Has there ever been a time when something happened unexpectedly? **Maybe your birthday party got rained out, or maybe the lights went out while you were at the grocery store.** Sometimes, something unexpected can occur while you're just playing around. It can even happen while you're playing basketball on a warm spring day.

It was sunny outside, and all the flowers were as **bright as a parrot's feathers.** The cool air, **which was unstirred by wind**, had a **light fragrance** of the **light morning dew. The dew shone vibrantly on the petals of the flowers**, for there were no clouds in the sky. "**Rrrrrrrrr!**" Our **garage door moaned**, for its hinges **needed to be oiled.**

"Toss me the ball," I called to my dad, "**it's a marvelous day!**"

"Are you ready to lose?" my **dad teased.**

"**You better watch out Dad!** I'm as ready as you are." I **responded.**

We began to **shoot** around for a while. My **shots were going in one after the other**. We played one round of "Around the World," and we did a little one on one. **Naturally**, I won the game, but I had a feeling that he was **going easy on me.**

"Do you want to take a break **April**?" Dad asked, "It's getting dark out."

"**Sure, but just a little one." I replied.**

As I sat down, I observed how dark it was. It was getting darker, and the **warmth of the sun was slowly fading away. It faded like a persnickity persons pretty smile as something sad happens.**

"Did you see how Kobe made that final shot in yesterday's game Dad?" I **questioned.**

"That was **awesome!**" Dad stated.

I stood up and started to bounce the ball. Dad stood **up and started** to walk towards the garage.

"Don't leave Dad!" I **pleaded.**

"It's getting dark." Dad **replied.**

"Just one more shot?" I **begged.**

"Okay!" Dad **responded.**

He watched me as I bounced the ball a few times to go for the shot. I ran, **one foot after the other**, bouncing the ball. I **leaped, and while I was in the air**, I spun around once in a complete circle. I shot it, **then "SWOOSH!"** I stood there stunned...It went in!

Dad hugged me and I said, "That was. . .amazing!"

After we picked up the ball, Dad and I went inside. My dad explained to my mom what had happened. I was shocked. I wasn't expecting to make that shot. **I don't know how I did it or how it went in. It was unexplainable.**

—Celeste Cardenas, grade 7

Score point 4. Rich language, effective dialogue and imagery contribute to this very effective piece.

Grade 7—Score Point 3

Has there ever been a time when something happened unexpectedly? Sometimes, something unexpected can occur while you're just playing around. It can even happen while you're playing **basketball on a warm spring day.**

It was sunny outside, and **all the flowers were blooming. The cool air smelled great.** There were no clouds in the sky. I opened the garage door **and it squeaked.**

"Toss me the ball," I called to my dad.

"Are you ready to lose?" my dad replied.

"I'm as ready as you are." I replied.

We began to play around for a while. We played one round of "Around the World," and we did a little one on one. I won the game, **but I had a feeling that he was letting me win.**

"Let's take a break. It's getting dark." Dad said.

I sat down, and I saw how dark it was. It was getting darker and darker.

"Did you see how Kobe made that final shot in yesterday's game?" I asked.
"It was good!" Dad said.

I stood up and I started to bounce the ball. Dad stood up. He started to walk towards the garage.

"Don't leave Dad!" I said.

"It's getting dark." Dad said

"Just one more shot?" I said.

"Okay!" Dad said.

He watched me as **I bounced the ball a few times to go for the shot.** I ran bouncing the ball. I jumped, **and I spun around once.** I shot it, and it went in the basket. I stood there **stunned.**

Dad hugged me and I **said, "That was amazing!"**

After we picked up the ball, Dad and I went inside. My dad explained to my mom what had happened. I was shocked. I wasn't expecting to make that shot.

Score point: 3. Though this paper has some repetition, the ideas are generally developed, with layering of internalized thoughts or "asides" along with the dialogue and action of this well-narrated memory.

For classroom duplication only. Enlarge at 121% for 81/2 x 11 sheet

144　　**Reviving The Essay** © 2005 Discover Writing Press • www.discoverwriting.com

Grade 7—Score Point 2

Sometimes, something unexpected can occur while you're just playing around. It can even happen while you're playing basketball.

It was sunny outside. There were no clouds in the sky. I opened the garage door. My dad told me to give him the ball and asked if I was ready to loose the game. I told him no. **We played one round of "Around the World," and we did a little one on one. I won the game.**

We took a break because it was getting dark. I stood up and I started to bounce the ball. Dad stood up. He started to walk towards the garage. I asked him not to leave because I wanted to play **a little longer.** He said OK, and we played **a little longer.**

He watched me bounce the ball. I ran bouncing the ball. I jumped, and shot it. It went in the basket. I was surprised. **My dad was surprised too, and he hugged me.**

After we picked up the ball, Dad and I went inside. My dad explained to my mom what had happened. **I was shocked. I wasn't expecting to make that shot.**

Score point: 2. Some gaps exist in this piece, causing abrupt shifts in focus. Ideas are presented in summarized, superficial form, almost as a sequenced list of events. The writer is successful, though, at conveying enough of the experience to let the reader see that the insightful beginning was skillful foreshadowing.

For classroom duplication only. Enlarge at 121% for 8 1/2 x 11 sheet

Reviving The Essay © 2005 Discover Writing Press • www.discoverwriting.com   **145**

Grade 7—Score Point 1

I'm going to tell you about a time I played basketball with my dad and something unexpected happened. I opened the garage door. **My dad** told me to give him the ball and asked if I was ready to loose the game. **We played** for a while. It started to get dark. **I started** to bounce the ball. Dad went in the house. **I asked** him not to leave because I wanted to play a little longer. He said OK, and we played a little longer. **He watched** me bounce the ball. **I jumped and shot it.**   It went in the basket. **I was** surprised.

We went inside after that and told my mom what happened.

Score point: 1. Simple and choppy sentence structures; abrupt shifts and gaps in development; lack of depth of ideas and voice impair reader involvement and overall effectiveness of the piece.

For classroom duplication only. Enlarge at 121% for 81/2 x 11 sheet

146   **Reviving The Essay** © 2005 Discover Writing Press • www.discoverwriting.com

Getting Ready for a Reader's Ears

Lesson 28:
Dogberry Logic

One of the most serious problems in student writing is repetitive ideas. Students might say they have three points to make, and then list the same point over and over, just paraphrased. For instance: "Football is a popular sport at my school," followed by, "Furthermore, people really like it," and then "The third point is that everyone goes to the games." What do all three of these statements mean? The same thing.

Students might know how to use transitional words, but what they're connecting isn't logical thought. There's no "movement of the mind," as Newkirk puts it. Just the same thought, recast and dressed up in transitions.

The real problem here is that students don't always distinguish between the sound of real thought progression and the sound of logical transition words linking illogical content. How do we teach this distinction to students in a way they will remember it? Just marking an essay with "this is repetitive" doesn't do it. Neither does it work to simply issue warnings, like "Don't forget….don't be repetitive, unless you choose to use it as an effect."

Barry Lane advocates going in a back door when there's resistance at the front door, and letting students experience their learning through humor. So this exercise is a fun way to raise student awareness of the above problem by showing them how *not* to write.

We have a mentor text handy, in a speech by Dogberry, a hilarious character in Shakespeare's *Much Ado About Nothing*. (In the most recent film version, the role was played by Michael Keaton.) Dogberry does the exact same thing with his speech (see excerpt below). Rather than show the speech to students, it's more effective to lead them through a paragraph-imitating exercise to have them experience it for themselves. The speech is great dessert afterward.

Teaching It:

1. Write an opinion statement that you've heard someone say. (It works well to use a compliment about one of their friends, like "Candice has pretty hair.") Look up when you're done.
2. On the next line, paraphrase that statement. Don't use any of the same words. Look up when you're done.
3. On the next line, again put that opinion in other words.
4. On the next and final line, paraphrase it one more time.
5. Now, in front of the second sentence, write the word *also*.
6. In front of the third sentence, write *however*.
7. In front of the last sentence, write *in conclusion*.
8. Read the whole thing aloud to a partner.
9. *(Share a few with the large group. Then, show a video clip of Michael Keaton in* Much Ado About Nothing, *or have volunteers read the excerpt printed below, so that students see the ludicrous logic and its humor.)*

Debriefing Questions:

1. What do you notice?

2. Why was that funny?

3. How would this have been different if you'd seen the model before you wrote?

4. Did anyone hear a paragraph that actually sounded pretty good? See how dangerous this problem is? You paraphrased the sentence as nearly as you could, yet it sounds to your ear like several different ideas.

Spin-offs:

Have everyone write a different opinion sentence. Put them into a hat, and draw those sentences to use in the exercise above, instead of one paraphrased sentence. (This is more effective for younger writers.)

Student Samples:

Carrie is sweet.
Also she isn't hateful.
However my neighbor seems very nice.
In conclusion my friend isn't as dreadful as she might seem at first.
  —Matilde, grade 7

My father could light up the room with his smile.
Also when dad looked at you, his eyes showed the joy he brought to others.
However he never knew a stranger where ever he went.
In conclusion Dad was the life of the party.
  —Sarah, grade 11

Don Pedro: Officers, what offence have these men done?

Dogberry: Marry, sir, they have committed false report; moreover, they have spoken untruths; secondarily, they are slanders; sixth and lastly, they have belied a lady; thirdly, they have verified unjust things; and to conclude, they are lying knaves.

Don Pedro: First, I ask thee what they have done; thirdly, I ask thee what's their offence; sixth and lastly, why they are committed; and, to conclude, what you lay to their charge.

—William Shakespeare, *Much Ado About Nothing* (Act V, Scene i)

For classroom duplication only. Enlarge at 121% for 81/2 x 11 sheet

150 **Reviving The Essay** © 2005 Discover Writing Press • www.discoverwriting.com

The following student sample shows a paper that failed because of Dogberry Logic:

There are lots of ways a person can impact your life. Someone in your family that you are really close to can make a big difference in how you live. Your future can be changed by a good friend, a relationship or it even could be death. For many reasons, other people could easily effect and impact your life. There's always something or someone that will impact your life like your mom or dad, or somebody else in your family that you are really close to and love very much. It might even be a lot of people. You could have really good friend that you spend a lot of time together, and that you care about. This person can change your life. You also might have a death in your family; that can change your life in many ways. There are so many examples of changes a person can make in another person's life. Also, most impacts and effects in a person's life also depend on what of person they are going to be in life. Many parts of a person's background can make a difference in how their life comes out in the future. It all depends on what kind of choices you make.

It also helps to think before you do something. One thing that you do wrong can change your life and other people's lives around you.

Throwaway Writing

Another common weakness in essays is known to us as "throwaway writing." This type of writing is common among novice writers who think it belongs there. In testing, it's a hallmark of mediocre scores. Here is how "throwaway writing" got its nickname:

> Overheard (paraphrased) conversation between an educator and one state high-stakes-testing essay-scoring official, at a scoring training venue:
>
> Teacher: What about this sentence?
>
> Psychometrician: Which sentence?
>
> Teacher: The beginning sentence on the essay, which reads, "I am going to tell you the good parts and the bad parts about a rainy day."
>
> Psychometrician: At that point, we're still waiting for the essay to kick in. We're still waiting for it to say something.
>
> Teacher: That first sentence doesn't show organization? As an introduction?
>
> Psychometrician: Nope. It's throwaway writing. We don't count it negatively or positively, we just keep reading and looking for the essay to begin.
>
> Teacher: Throwaway?
>
> Psychometrician: Yep. It's space that the writer could've used for something else.

Writing teachers can easily name sentences or phrases that are clearly throwaway writing. This exercise provides a lighthearted way for students to play with how not to write an essay, by loading it down with throwaway writing. And afterward, students will be able to identify throwaway writing and prevent it, too.

Teaching It:

Today we're going to focus on something called "throwaway writing." Listen to this, and see if you can tell me what throwaway writing you hear.

(Read the first paragraph of Cyndi Pina's "My Paper," below.)

Who can tell me one part that you consider throwaway?

(List phrases on a poster, like "In my paper I am going to tell you" and "this concludes my introduction.")

Can you think of any other phrases like this that writers sometimes use?

(Add other thoughts to the poster, like "Hi, my name is…" and "I am going to tell you the good things and the bad things…" and "Thank you for reading my paper."

Let's read a little more of this essay. Listen for any throwaway parts you hear.

(Almost the entire paper is throwaway, so let them pick out more phrases for the wall poster.)

Some people think that phrases like these are good in an essay, but they're really not. Think about it. Do people ever really talk like this?

Now, here is your challenge. You are going to have five minutes to write one of the following: a thank-you note, a 911 phone call, or a love note. The trick is to put in as many of these phrases from this poster as possible.

Share aloud.

Debriefing Questions:

1. Do people do throwaway talking? Why?

2. Is throwaway writing a necessary first step in getting thoughts on paper?

3. What function does it serve? What else might serve the same function?

4. Is there any such thing as throwaway teaching? What does it sound like?

My Paper

This is the introduction of my paper. In my paper I am going to tell you about the beginning, the middle, and the end. I believe that these parts of my paper are very important which is why I am telling you that I believe in their validity. My three reasons for writing this paper are my beliefs in this issue, my three reasons for this issue, and my opinion about this issue. This concludes my introduction.

Now I am finished with the introduction. This sentence is the transition of my paper where I flow from the beginning of my paper to the middle of my paper. I am now going to tell you what I told you I was going to tell you. First of all, my beliefs in this issue are very, very, very strong because I firmly believe in them. For example, my previous statement clearly reflects my belief in the importance of this issue. "My beliefs in this issue are very, very, very strong because I firmly believe in them." This point has now been proved.

Secondly, my three reasons (as mentioned above) are the beginning, the middle, and the end. These are important elements in any paper. Without these basic elements I would not be able to tell you what I am going to tell you, what I am telling you, and what I told you (although I haven't told you anything yet). This is my third transitional sentence.

Thirdly, I will now focus on my final argument. My opinion belongs to me; therefore, it is my most powerful argument. It is my opinion that my beliefs and reasons on this issue are extremely important which is why I have chosen this topic. This is the last transitional sentence. (Whew!)

IN CONCLUSION, I would like to furthermore add my grand finale. This is where I tell you what I have told you. I have written this paper because of my beliefs in this issue, my three reasons for this issue, and my opinion about this issue; thus, concluding my paper. The End.

—Cyndi Piña, 9th and 11th grade teacher

Student Samples:

Dear John,

I am writing to tell you three reasons about why I love you. In this letter, you will hear what I love about you, how much I love you, and what I hope you will say to me after you read this letter. I hope you enjoy the letter. Thank you for reading it.

Sincerely,

Margo

Uh...hello, 9-1-1?   In this phone call I will tell you about an emergency happening in my house right at this moment. I will tell you the good and the bad things about fires in the living room. First, I will cover the bad things. Smoke is bad. Next, the heat from the flames is also bad. Third, the house will be expensive to replace. This concludes my 9-1-1 phone call.

Lesson 30:
I Want to Show You Something

Sometimes students have strange ideas about what their writing is supposed to accomplish. Sometimes they have mysterious notions about what "good writing" looks like or sounds like. It helps to clarify all of these questions by considering what good writing does.

Good writing lets a reader slip into the skin of the writer and vicariously experience something. The short drama below provides a clear view of the writer's relationship and responsibility to the reader. The teacher performs the role of Person A, and a volunteer (usually a student) is Person B. It helps to practice it with the volunteer before presenting it.

Though it's clearly very simplified, the four "ways" demonstrated in the scene below are representations of the four score points on a four-point rubric.

Teaching It:

We're going to demonstrate something for you in four different ways. Just watch and see what you notice. We'll ask you to talk about it after the fourth one, so please hold your thoughts until then. Ready?

A: *(to audience)* Here comes the first way.
(B covers both eyes with hands and stands perfectly still.)
A: *(to B)* I want to show you something! *(A marches around, pausing and pointing at various things, then walks back over to B.)* What do you think?
B: **Huh?** *(They freeze briefly, then return to starting point.)*

A: *(to audience)* Here comes the second way.
(B covers one eye with hand and stands still, watching with the one uncovered eye.)
A: *(to B)* I want to show you something! *(A marches around, pausing and pointing at various things, then walks back over to B.)* What do you think?
B: **Okay ...** *(They freeze, then return to starting point.)*

A: *(to audience)* Here comes the third way.
(B uncovers both eyes.)
A: *(to B)* I want to show you something! *(A links her arm to B, and then walks B around, pausing and pointing at various things. Then she stops and turns to B.)* What do you think?
B: **Ahhh.** *(Freeze, then return to starting point.)*

A: *(to audience)* Here comes the fourth way.
A: *(to B)* I want to show you something! *(A moves behind B, raises B's arm and whispers to B to point a finger. A then uses B's arm to point at various things, then stops.)* What do you think?
B: **Wow!** *(Both freeze.)*

Debriefing Questions:

1. What happened first? second? third? fourth? (Students describe what they saw.)

2. Could the follower see? (In varying degrees.) Did the leader want her to? (Yes, each time.)

3. What did this have to do with writing? Who were these people? (A writer and a reader.)

4. What does this tell us about what the writer needs to keep in mind? (The experience of the reader.)

5. How can a writer put the reader "in his shoes"? What are some ways? (List on the wall skills we already have that make a reader slip into the skin of the writer; skills we use that help the writer experience that fourth way, instead of the first or second way.)

Student samples, which demonstrates the 4th way:

Toys R Us and Home Depot
Ashley Chambers, grade 8

I love to laugh, so did he. I dream of fame and fortune, so did he. He enjoyed playing with wood and "big people toys." I loved my toys too. The similarities are almost frightening. This man that I seem to be mirroring is my dad. We always shared many of the same personality characteristics. However, one of these traits sticks out in my mind. We both loved to go on spur of the moment shopping sprees. Even though he would buy tools and I would buy toys, the fact of the matter still remains that we loved to spend our money. On rare occasions, my piggy bank would begin to look a little full, or sometimes my dad would notice he had some extra cash lying around. Almost instinctively we would go as soon as possible and contribute to the economy by handing our money to the nearest cashier in exchange for some item we'd been dreaming about.

For very deserving reasons, these adventures to lose our money were called our "Toys R Us and Home Depot runs." Somehow these little errands always ended up lasting all day.

First, my dad would take off all the doors and cover on his old jeep before my mom would notice. His beat up jeep was one of those antiques that you were able to remove all the doors and walls and pretty soon you'd just be left with the frame of the car. My mom thought it was too dangerous for me to be riding in a car like this. So we would sneak out of the driveway before she would notice. Before I knew it I saw the familiar sign that read, "Toys R Us."

Once we were in the cold building, my dad would rush me up and down a couple of aisles. Even though I wasn't ready to make any final purchases, my dad would grab the closest toy or game an anxiously mumble, "Come on Ash, look at this game. It's perfect. Now let's go." "But Daddy, you've never seen that game before." "Umm...Oh...of course I have. Now let's go pay the lady." There was no use trying. I gave my pathetic plea as I was unwillingly dragged to the check out.

Pretty soon we were back in the old jeep and I curiously stared at some toy that I knew neither of us had any about what it was or how it worked. As the wheels of the beat up jeep turned, we ended up back on the road, heading for my dad's favorite place: Home Depot. Normally my dad was a very cautious driver, going at least a couple of miles under the speed limit. But oddly enough, when we were

For classroom duplication only. Enlarge at 121% for 81/2 x 11 sheet

on our way to Home Depot he would actually make the old engine in his jeep creep up to the speed limit. For my dad that was pretty risky.

Once the big orange sign finally came into view through the scratched windshield, it seemed like all that built up anxiety suddenly rushed out of my dad and he grew completely calm, so calm that several times we missed our exit on the highway.

As the clear glass windows opened and I felt the cool breeze that smelled like wood chips, I looked up and saw a big smile spread across my dad's thrilled face. It was like watching a young kid walk into their favorite candy store. Then we began our great journey up and down every single cold, cement aisle. We'd walk, race, and talk about anything and everything. I would tell him all the latest kindergarten gossip and then he would try to explain to me how football was played.

After what seemed like hours, I began to grow weary. However, my dad wasn't quite ready to go yet. "Umm, I'm not quit ready yet, Ash. Look at all this stuff! How neat is this? Just a couple more minutes and then we'll head on home."

"Okay Daddy," I would reply, even though I knew it would be a while longer before we left. So I would either climb up into the cart or hop into my dad's arms. After I was comfortably seated, I would usually fall asleep or start asking my dad a bunch of pressing questions. Eventually, he would find something he couldn't live without. As we finally approached the checkout counter my dad would tell me, "Now if Mom asks how much this cost, tell her that Daddy and Uncle Pudge split it." "Ok Daddy," I responded as usual. It just so happened that when dad would tell me this fib, he was usually buying something fairly expensive and I knew that my mom wouldn't be too happy with the cost.

Before I knew it, we climbed back out of the jeep with some huge tool or machine in the back seat. Meanwhile, on the drive home my dad was back to being the slowest driver on the road and humming some old song I hadn't heard of,

Finally, the jeep would pull into the driveway and we walked into the front door. We smelled the burnt scent of my mom trying to cook some new recipe. My dad and I would run to the table and sit down. Even though my mom wasn't the most talented cook, after a long day of shopping we would eat anything. Once we were seated, my Mom would ask my Dad and me about our "errands." I would tell her about my toy and then she would cunningly ask, "So what did your Daddy get?"

"Oh...umm...he got this new tool. Oh but don't worry, Uncle Pudge and him split it." I saw my dad begin to snicker at the other end of the table, because even as a little kid I was a horrible liar.

For classroom duplication only. Enlarge at 121% for 81/2 x 11 sheet

Reviving The Essay © 2005 Discover Writing Press • www.discoverwriting.com   **159**

Christmas Eve, 9:00, Granddad's bed time, farmers go to bed early to wake up early. Granddad always says early to bed, early to rise. Christmas Eve at my Granddad's house is always the same. Everyone is in bed by 9:15 to wake up to the smell of bacon and eggs with biscuits and gravy, my grandma's specialty. So my aunts and uncles went to their rooms leaving all the kids on the cold couches in the living room. Me, I'm not a heavy sleeper and can't fall asleep with the heater crackling in my ear, right next to my couch. My couch is old, pink, with green flower-like design on it. I'm one of the smaller ones. Leaving me with the smallest couch doesn't leave my cousins feeling bad. The year was 1995, and I was 7 years old. In my eyes I was old enough to know better, but still too young to care. I was a pretty quick kid. People make an impact in your life every day, you have to be smart enough to notice them.

I got up from my couch and sat Indian style on the cold tile floor to warm my little body. I was a tanned boy with golden brown hair. My Grandma called me her "Golden Boy." In the back of my mind I remembered that my grandma had made chocolate pudding. I got up and walked across the cold tile floor that almost felt like it was burning my small feet. I quickly opened the refrigerator and tried not to wake anybody. I reached in and grabbed the pudding. I closed the refrigerator and reached with my weak arms into the clean dishes in the left part of the sink. A chill went through me when I picked up the freezing spoon. I walked over to the big oval shaped table and sat at the end where my Granddad perpetually sits at every meal. I have always wanted to be just like him, pretty big shoes to fill; since I can remember he has always been my hero, the man that could never die.

I took a few bites out of my chocolate heaven when I heard a low pitched click, I knew who and what it was. Unusually my Granddad was up and he had locked the bathroom door. You see, the bathroom is connected to his bedroom and the table is right outside both of them, and with the thin, rotten, wooden walls in the pristine house you can hear anything that makes the smallest noises. Even my little feet slapping across the tile floor could be heard, had someone been listening.

From inside the bathroom I heard a rattling noise like pills in a little bottle. I could almost vision him in front of the sink, a cup of warm water, taking a pill for his heart problems. All at once I stopped eating the pudding and sucked on my spoon. I began to think about the next morning when I heard a fist hit the wall from inside the bathroom. I got scared hoping, wishing someone would wake up to help. No one did. I could hear him gasping for air inside the bathroom. I twisted the handle it was locked. I stabbed the long end of the spoon into the crack of the door where I could see light, and it unlocked. With my weak innocent arms I through the door opened and looked inside. It was my most feared imaginable thing possible. My hero not breathing on the bathroom floor with one hand in the dry tub and the other holding the empty tube of pills palm up I did the only thing I knew to do. I quickly got next to him on the floor and yelled at the top of my lungs. "Help !!!" All at once lights came on in the house. Everyone filled up the bathroom to see me hugging my granddaddy's chest with tears running down my red face and soaking his white t-shirt. I had never been so scared in my life, I was just a boy.

My dad and two of my uncles, in nothing but their Christmas pajamas carried my granddad to the truck and took off to the hospital. Me and my grandmother followed them. When we got there it was close to 2 o'clock in the morning, Christmas Day. My mother really didn't want me to go, but I didn't give her much of a choice. I slept in the chair next to my granddad's hospital bed. When I woke up Christmas morning to a beeping noise I had a gray, itchy hospital blanket, and a white sheeted pillow to lay my head down on. I looked over not really aware of where I was and saw my granddad on a long skinny bed with a white hospital gown on. My eyes began to swell up until I saw the monitor with his heartbeat showing. I stood on the chair, kissed his forehead and whispered "Merry Christmas." I saw a tear roll down his dry red face. The doctor came in and I wiped the tear away. He told me if we had gotten there any later he wouldn't be breathing right now. He also said I was a bright boy.

My granddad told me that no one had ever done something for him that meant as much as what I had done. My hero died this past Christmas left me knowing that no one else would make as big an impact on me or my life as he did. I just hope he will be waiting for me when my day comes so we can spend it in paradise.

—Travis M Moncus, grade 10

Appendix

The pages in this appendix can serve as reproducible handouts, posters, or transparencies.

The first pages illustrate the steps for writing an essay and make handy reminders during the writing process. Some teachers create classroom posters similar to them, using pieces of their own students' writing.

The collection of alternative text structures can be copied and cut up for use as transparencies or as manipulatives for students to browse through as they "shop for a structure."

The song parodies have been included because many teachers like to "pump up the energy" in a classroom by surprising students with an unexpected performance, especially to break the tension in the days before a high-stakes test.

For classroom duplication only. Enlarge at 121% for 81/2 x 11 sheet

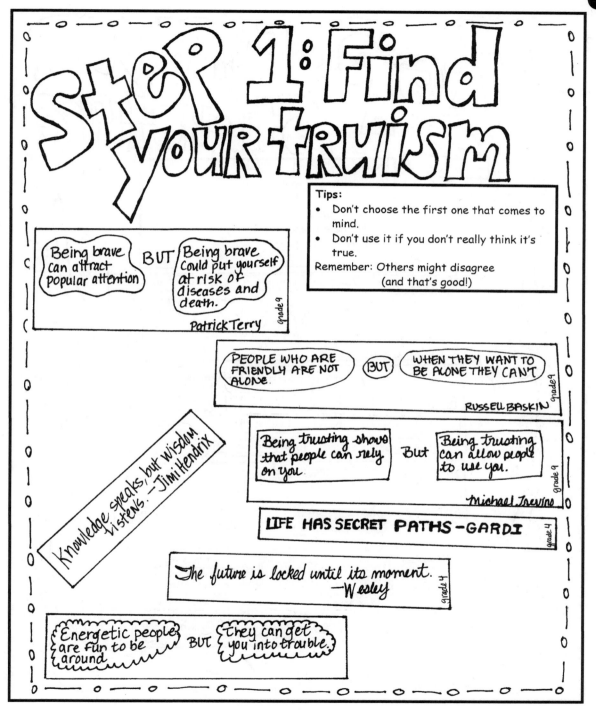

Step 1: Find your truism

Tips:
- Don't choose the first one that comes to mind.
- Don't use it if you don't really think it's true.

Remember: Others might disagree
(and that's good!)

Being brave can attract popular attention **BUT** Being brave could put yourself at risk of diseases and death.

Patrick Terry grade 9

PEOPLE WHO ARE FRIENDLY ARE NOT ALONE. BUT WHEN THEY WANT TO BE ALONE THEY CAN'T

RUSSELL BASKIN grade 9

Knowledge speaks, but wisdom listens. —Jimi Hendrix

Being trusting shows that people can rely on you. But Being trusting can allow people to use you.

Michael Trevino grade 9

LIFE HAS SECRET PATHS —GARDI grade 4

The future is locked until its moment. —Wesley grade 4

Energetic people are fun to be around BUT they can get you into trouble.

For classroom duplication only. Enlarge at 121% for 8 1/2 x 11 sheet

Reviving The Essay © 2005 Discover Writing Press • www.discoverwriting.com   **165**

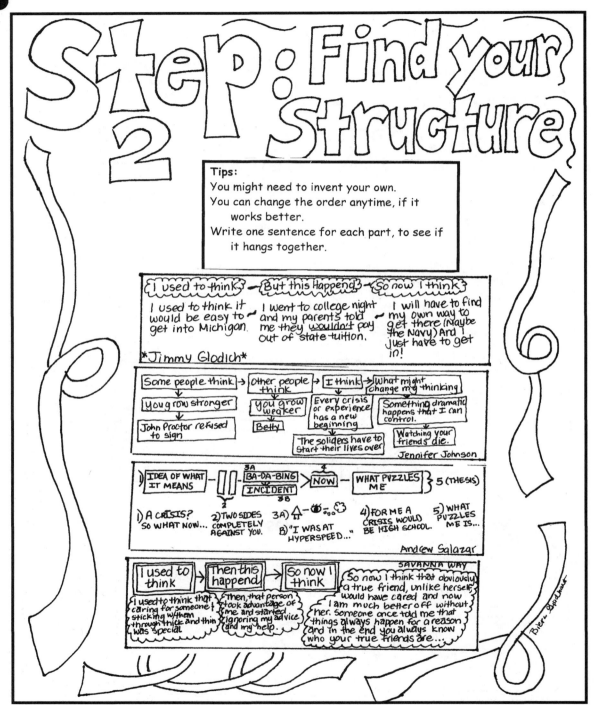

Step 2: Find your Structure

Tips:
You might need to invent your own.
You can change the order anytime, if it works better.
Write one sentence for each part, to see if it hangs together.

I used to think — But this Happened — So now I think

I used to think it would be easy to get into Michigan.

I went to college night and my parents told me they wouldn't pay out of state tuition.

I will have to find my own way to get there (Maybe the Navy) And I just have to get in!

Jimmy Glodich

Some people think → Other people think → I think → What might change my thinking

you grow stronger

you grow weaker

Every crisis or experience has a new beginning

Something dramatic happens that I can control.

John Proctor refused to sign

Betty

The soliders have to start their lives over

Watching your friends die.

Jennifer Johnson

1) IDEA OF WHAT IT MEANS — 3A BA-DA-BING INCIDENT 3B — NOW — WHAT PUZZLES ME — 5 (THESIS)

1) A CRISIS? SO WHAT NOW... 2) TWO SIDES COMPLETELY AGAINST YOU. 3A) B) "I WAS AT HYPERSPEED..." 4) FOR ME A CRISIS WOULD BE HIGH SCHOOL. 5) WHAT PUZZLES ME IS...

Andrew Salazar

I used to think → Then this happened → So now I think

SAVANNA WAY

I used to think that caring for someone, sticking with them through thick and thin was special.

Then, that person took advantage of me and started ignoring my advice and my help.

So now I think that obviously a true friend, unlike herself, would have cared and now I am much better off without her. Someone once told me that things always happen for a reason and in the end you always know who your true friends are...

For classroom duplication only. Enlarge at 121% for 81/2 x 11 sheet

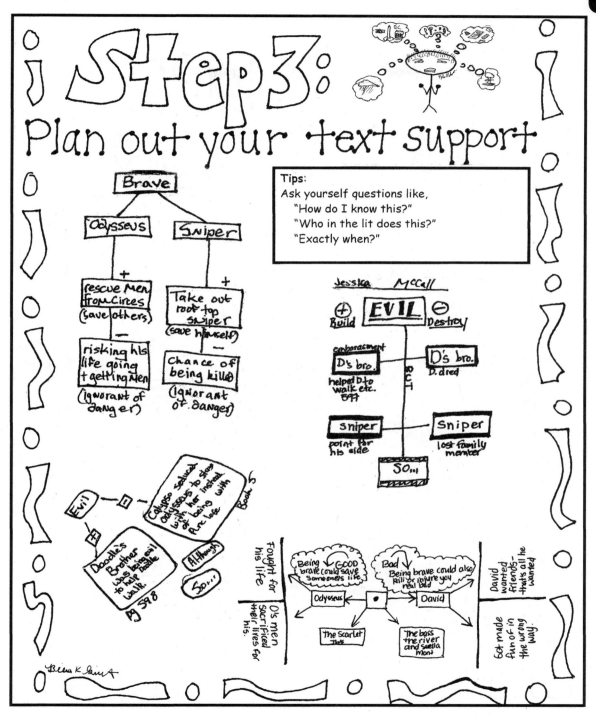

Step 3:
Plan out your text support

Tips:
Ask yourself questions like,
  "How do I know this?"
  "Who in the lit does this?"
  "Exactly when?"

Brave
- Odysseus
  - + rescue Men from Circes (save others)
  - − risking his life going t getting Men (ignorant of danger)
- Sniper
  - + Take out roof top sniper (save himself)
  - − Chance of being killd (ignorant of danger)

Jessica McCall

⊕ Build   EVIL   ⊖ Destroy

- caharacment / D's bro. helped D to walk etc. B97
- D's bro. D. dred
- Sniper point for his side
- Sniper lost family member
- So...

Evil / Calypso seduced Odysseus to stay with her instead of being with Pure love. Book 5
+ Doodle's Brother was being evil to help Doodle walk. Pg B98
Although / So...

Fought for his life
Being ↓ GOOD brave could save someones life
Bad ↓ Being brave could also kill or injure you real bad
Odysseus ◆ David
D's men sacrificied their lives for his.
The Scarlet This
The bass the river and suella Mont
David wanted friends — thats all he wanted
Got made fun of in the wrong way.

For classroom duplication only. Enlarge at 121% for 8 1/2 x 11 sheet

Reviving The Essay © 2005 Discover Writing Press • www.discoverwriting.com   **167**

Step 4: DRAFT IT!

Tips:
Pretend you're explaining it to someone and write down what you would say.

Pretend they're doubtful, and use 'pick-a-punk.'

Kim Goss
English 1-7
12/14/03

Good or Bad?

Many people in the world are friendly, but there are in friendly people I am talking about are in books. For instance in the sad, yet wonderful of "The Scarlet Ibis" Doodle's brother (the narrator) is a friendly person because he is helping Doodle by telling him, "All you got to do is try." (568) so that Doodle will feel encouraged and try Doodle's brother is also friendly because he helps Doodle. "I'm going to teach you to walk." (568), even though everyone says that Doodle can't.

The friendliness of the narrator is also a bad thing. One reason is that his friendliness causes him to push Doodle so hard that it eventually causes the death of poor Doodle. "I lay there crying, shattering my fallen scarlet ibis from the heresy of rain." (604)

Another good thing about being friendly is, you make a lot of friends. Just like Odysseus, from the famous, action-adventure tale The Odyssey, "Alcinous gives a banquet in honor of Odysseus." (893). In the many friends that Odysseus makes on his journey he tells them, "Friendship will bind us, though my land lies far." (896)

Odysseus's friendliness however gets him into trouble as well. Like when they meet the cyclops, Odysseus tries to be friendly, but it does no good with the

cyclopes. "Neither reply nor pity came from him, but in one stride he clutched at my companions and made his meal." (983)"

So being friendly could be good or bad depending on the situation. I can also a friendly person and because of that I have lots of friends. One time however I was so friendly that someone took advantage of me and my friendliness to hurt my feelings. All I know is that friendliness should be used in a good way by every person in the world. If that were so the world would be a better place... for all of us.

Works Cited

Applebee, Author, ed. The Language of Literature. Evanstone, McDougal Littell, 2000

Ben Drouillard

For classroom duplication only. Enlarge at 121% for 8 1/2 x 11 sheet

STEP 5: Design your Frame

Tips:
Play with the dialogue, lyrics, familiar words, quotations, story pieces, echoed phrases.

For classroom duplication only. Enlarge at 121% for 81/2 x 11 sheet

Reviving The Essay © 2005 Discover Writing Press • www.discoverwriting.com 169

Step 6: Try it on a reader's ears!

Tips:
Don't let them see it... just HEAR it.
Get a reaction... watch for:
            Huh?   Ok...   Ahh...   Wow!

Lauren Potts   Editor Nadja Padron

Peer Editing Checklist
Directions: You read your paper aloud to a partner. They should then fill out your "hearing it" section.
Your partner then reads his/her paper to you. You should fill out their "hearing it" section.
Then trade papers, and fill out the "seeing it" section for each other. Sign your partner's paper.

Hearing it:
✓ What's the whole idea of this paper?
    That hard times don't neccesarily show your inner spirit
    but show your personality instead
✓ What words or phrases did you find most thought-provoking?
    Do you think you know me?

✓ Circle one main reaction you'd summarize with: Huh?   Okay.   Ahhh.   **(Wow.)**

★ Great paper! what a wonderful vocabulary Awesome Job!

Hearing it:
    What's the whole idea of this paper?
    TRUTH WILL SHOW THROUGH WEATHER YOU SHOW YOUR FEELINGS
    OR TRY TO HIDE THEM
    What words or phrases did you find most thought-provoking?
    THE WAY YOU PUT THE QUOTES TOGETHER IN THE SENTENCE...
    "BEING SHOT AT IS NO FUN."
    Circle one main reaction you'd summarize with: Huh?   Okay.   Ahhh.   **(Wow.)**

Hearing it:
✓ What's the whole idea of this paper?
    Evil could be good or bad.

    What words or phrases did you find most thought-provoking?
    Though this is primarily true, sometimes the way someone precieves...

    Circle one main reaction you'd summarize with: Huh?   Okay.   Ahhh.   **(Wow.)**

Hearing it:
    What's the whole idea of this paper?
    How a crisis can destroy you or make you stronger
    What words or phrases did you find most thought-provoking?
    They kingdom come...
    Circle one main reaction you'd summarize with: Huh?   Okay.   **(Ahhh.)**   Wow.

MORE TIPS
If you don't get
"ahh" and "wow,"
add Ba-da-bings
and more brushstrokes!

Hearing it:
✓ What's the whole idea of this paper?
    The way people look at any situation determines for
✓ themselves whats good or evil or wrong or right.
    What words or phrases did you find most thought-provoking?
    Reality is, therefore, objective because its based mostly
    on people's perceptions.
    Circle one main reaction you'd summarize with: Huh?   Okay.   Ahhh.   **(Wow?)**

Very Interesting! Nice Work.

Improving it: Read your paper, and find several spots to revise sentences into Ba-da-bings.
and staple them to the draft.

Bria K. Potts

Step 7: Make it ready for a reader's eyes!

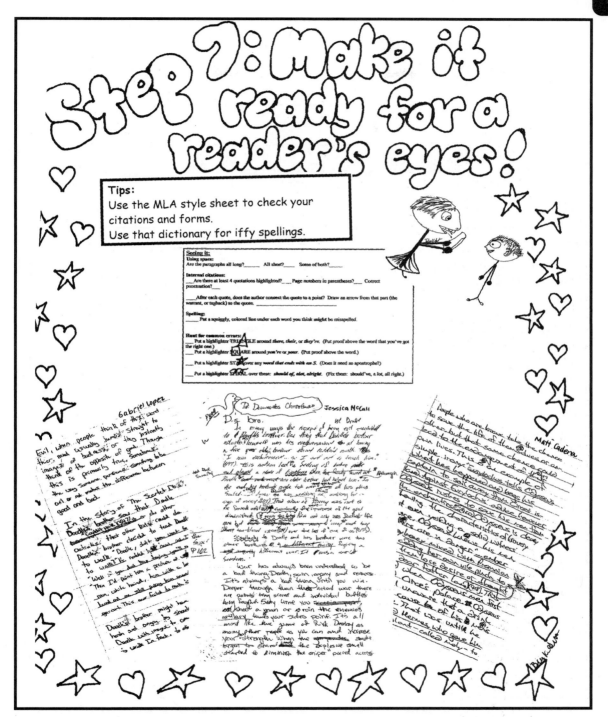

Tips:
Use the MLA style sheet to check your citations and forms.
Use that dictionary for iffy spellings.

Seeing it:

Using space:
Are the paragraphs all long?_____ All short?_____ Some of both?_____

Internal citations:
____ Are there at least 4 quotations highlighted?____ Page numbers in parentheses?____ Correct punctuation?_____

____ After each quote, does the author connect the quote to a point? Draw an arrow from that part (the warrant, or tagback) to the quote. _____

Spelling:
____ Put a squiggly, colored line under each word you think might be misspelled.

Hunt for common errors:
____ Put a highlighter TRIANGLE around *there*, *their*, or *they're*. (Put proof above the word that you've got the right one.)
____ Put a highlighter SQUARE around *you're* or *your*. (Put proof above the word.)
____ Put a highlighter STAR over any *word that ends with an S*. (Does it need an apostrophe?)
____ Put a highlighter SPIRAL over these: *should of*, *alot*, *alright*. (Fix them: should've, a lot, all right.)

For classroom duplication only. Enlarge at 121% for 8 1/2 x 11 sheet

Text Structures: Alternatives to the Schoolified Essay
A Growing Collection

A Memory

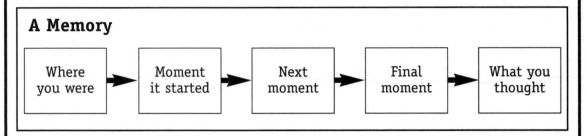

Where you were → Moment it started → Next moment → Final moment → What you thought

A Colorized Memory

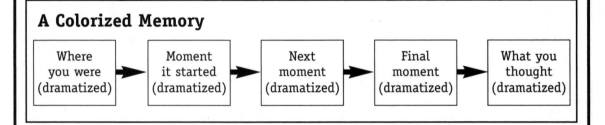

Where you were (dramatized) → Moment it started (dramatized) → Next moment (dramatized) → Final moment (dramatized) → What you thought (dramatized)

A Completely Made-up Story

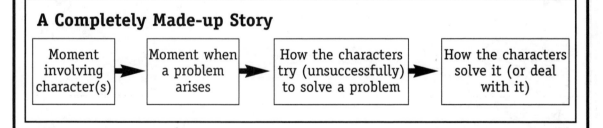

Moment involving character(s) → Moment when a problem arises → How the characters try (unsuccessfully) to solve a problem → How the characters solve it (or deal with it)

A Fable

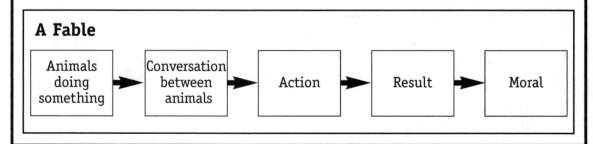

Animals doing something → Conversation between animals → Action → Result → Moral

For classroom duplication only. Enlarge at 121% for 81/2 x 11 sheet

Sequel to a Fable

| Moral of original fable | → | But the next day the animals said | → | And this happened | → | The result was | → | New moral |

Comparing Notes (Mine and Others')

| Some people think | → | other people think | → | I think | → | what could change my thinking |

Tevye's Debate

| On one hand | → | On the other hand | → | But on the other hand | → | But on the other hand | → | How I can be guided when the choice is so tough |

Evolution of a Term (word or phrase in the prompt)

| What the word meant to me when I was 4 | → | What the word meant to me when I was 10 | → | What the word means to me now | → | What the word will probably mean when I am _____ (pick an age) |

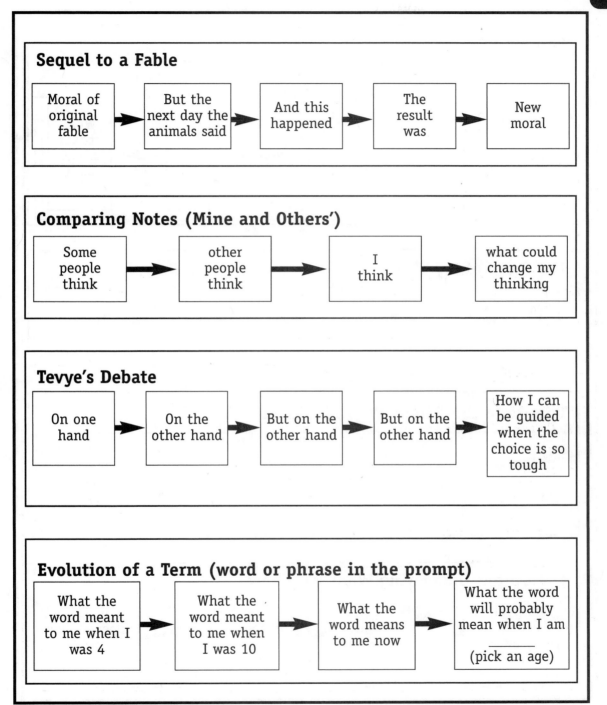

For classroom duplication only. Enlarge at 121% for 81/2 x 11 sheet

Spin of a Coin: Finding the Paradox

Two sides of the coin		How they are true in a fiction character		How they are true in a character in history		
How the thought is true	How the opposite is also true					What strikes me as most puzzling

The Story of My Thinking

What I used to think	but this happened	so now I think

Tribute to the Person Who Taught Me Something

What the lesson is	Flashback to the lesson	Description of the person	Lyrics or words you can remember that person saying (on any subject)	What I wish I could find out now from that person

The Onion: Unlayering What We Know

One (real) belief, something I know	How do I know this? (Tell one way you know)	If that had not happened, how else would you know it?	If that had not happened, how else would you know it?

For classroom duplication only. Enlarge at 121% for 81/2 x 11 sheet

Insight Garden

An insight about life	One illustration from literature	One illustration from a movie	An illustration from my life	I wonder

Mining for Raw Materials

The meaning of the statement

Recent conversation snippets

Evidence from stories

Objects (like Forrest Gump's white feather)

Ancient history

Sound effects

Lyrics

Personal experience

Movies

Current events

Haunting question

After mining, expand at least one fully (or more than one), then shape and design the framing or ribboning.

TBF (To be found)

For classroom duplication only. Enlarge at 121% for 8 1/2 x 11 sheet

Reviving The Essay © 2005 Discover Writing Press • www.discoverwriting.com   **175**

Steps for Writing a Good Essay

STEP 0: UNDERSTAND THE WRITING PROMPT.
Tips: Use the dictionary for any words you have questions about.
Look at the prompt from all angles.

STEP 1: FIND YOUR TRUISM.
Tips: Don't choose the first one that comes to mind.
Don't use it if you really don't think it's true.

STEP 2: FIND YOUR STRUCTURE.
Tips: You might need to invent your own.
You can change the order at any time.
Write one sentence for each part, to see if it hangs together.

STEP 3: PLAN OUT YOUR TEXT SUPPORT.
Tips: Your support can be not only from literature, but from your life.
Ask yourself questions like   "How do I know this?"
                                            "Who in the literature does this?"
                                            "Exactly when?"

STEP 4: DRAFT IT.
Tips: Pretend you're explaining it to someone and write what you'd say.
Pretend that other person is doubtful and you have to make it clear.

STEP 5: DESIGN YOUR FRAME.
Tips: Play with dialogue, lyrics, familiar words, quotations, story pieces, echoed phrases.

STEP 6: TRY IT ON A READER'S EARS.
Tips: Imagine that they can't see it, they can just hear it.
Try to get a reaction. Watch for: Huh? Okay! Ahhhh... Wow!!!!

STEP 7: MAKE IT READY FOR A READER'S EYES.
Tips: Use the dictionary for iffy spellings.
Check your citations and forms.

For classroom duplication only. Enlarge at 121% for 81/2 x 11 sheet

The following three song parodies were contributed by Carrie Strmiska, part of a group of dynamic Round Rock teachers who regularly delight their students by singing to them!

Write, Write, Baby!
(to the tune of "Ice, Ice Baby" by Vanilla Ice)
Carrie Strmiska, Round Rock ISD

All right, STOP, elaborate and listen...
4th grade is back with a brand new convention.
Someone, grip a pencil tightly,
Writing compositions daily and nightly.
Will it ever stop? YO! I hope no!
Turn off the lights and we'll glow.
To the extreme we rock a prompt like a vandal,
Light up a page, illuminate like a candle.
DANCE! I like the words that move,
They're fun to read and make writing smooth.
DEADLY! When we use those similes—
Sharp as a tack—makes me happy!
Love it or hate it—you write anyway!
The prompt's not our choice, but write well, okay?
If it is a problem, YO! we'll solve it!
Check out our skills as our writers compose it!
WRITE, WRITE, BABY...

For classroom duplication only. Enlarge at 121% for 81/2 x 11 sheet

Reviving The Essay © 2005 Discover Writing Press • www.discoverwriting.com   **177**

I Will Revise (to the tune of "I Will Survive" by Donna Summer)
Carrie Strmiska, Round Rock ISD

At first I was afraid, I was petrified
It's so hard to fill a paper with just two sides.
So I spent so many days just a tryin' to figure out,
I finally did—what fourth grade writing's all about

And we practiced all that we knew—
Ideas, details, support, leads, and conclusions, too
We are great writers. We've known that all along,
and we grew strong. Now we're at Camp Write Along.

Oh there I go, I wrote a four.
You won't believe it. It's much better than before.
Can you believe how much it changed since I revised?
It has more sparkle. Now you know why I revise.

And I know I, I will revise
I go back and check my paper with a careful eye
I've got many words to use,
metaphors, similes to choose,
I will revise, I will revise, hey, hey

When I read that lead again, I had to change
that part.
Description, dialogue, and questions—man that
choice was hard.
Or would that short sentence now catch my
reader's eye....
In the end, which conclusion would they buy?

And we practice writing great plans—
well thought out details, so the reader understands.
If we check the prompt and plan we know we won't
go wrong,
We are the campers, the campers of
Camp Write Along.

Oh there I go, I wrote a four.
You won't believe it. It's much better than before.
Can you believe how much it changed since I revised?
It has more sparkle. Now you know why I revise.

And I know I, I will revise
I go back and check my paper with a careful eye
I've got many words to use,
metaphors, similes to choose,
I will revise, I will revise, hey, hey

Oh there I go, I wrote a four.
You won't believe it. It's much better than before.
Can you believe how much it changed since I revised?
It has more sparkle. Now you know why I revise.

And I know I, I will revise
I must go back and check my paper with a careful eye
I've got many words to use,
metaphors, similes to choose,
I will revise, I will revise, hey, hey

For classroom duplication only. Enlarge at 121% for 81/2 x 11 sheet

Edit (To the tune of "Beat It")
by Tom Russian

Say develop ideas and organize here
Don't wanna see mistakes, they better disappear
I read it with my eyes, and the words are really clear!
So Edit, Just Edit

You better look, you better see what you can
Don't wanna see no wrong, don't be an error man
Need to write enough, better do what you can
So Edit, you don't wanna be sad
(Chorus)
Just Edit, Edit, Edit, Edit
Which word needs to be deleted?
Showin' how funky, strong is your writer
It doesn't matter with your first write
Just Edit, Edit   Just Edit, Edit
Just Edit, Edit   Just Edit, Edit

TAKS out to get you, better write what you can
Don't wanna get a one, let's be a writing fan
You wanna get a four, better do what you can
So Edit, just Edit

You have to show them that you're really not scared
You're writing for your life, I know you really care
They'll rate you, then they score you
Then they tell you it's fair
So Edit, You don't wanna be sad

Works Cited

Aesop's Fables: Online Collection. 6 May 2001 <http://www.aesopfables.com>

Atwell, Nancie. 1998. *In the Middle: New Understanding About Writing, Reading, and Learning.* Portsmouth, N.H.: Heinemann.

Bakhtin, M. M. 1981. *The Dialogic Imagination: Four Essays.* Austin: University of Texas Press.

———. 1986. *Speech Genres & Other Late Essays.* Austin: University of Texas Press.

Bernabei, Gretchen. 1992. "What Sixth Graders Learn from the Journal of Bobby G." *English Journal* 81.5 (September): 78–80.

———. 2003. *Lightning in a Bottle.* San Antonio: Trail of Breadcrumbs.

Bradbury, Ray. 1990. *Zen in the Art of Writing: Releasing the Creative Genius Within You.* New York: Bantam Books.

Brock, Paula. 2002. *Nudges.* Spring, Tex.: Absey & Co.

Burke, Jim. 2001. *Illuminating Texts: How to Teach Students to Read the World.* Portsmouth, N.H.: Heinemann.

Call for Manuscripts, "Cases: English Teachers at Work." 1991. *The English Journal.* NCTE.

Carroll, Joyce Armstrong. 2002. *Dr. JAC's Guide to Writing with Depth.* Spring, Tex.: Absey & Co.

Cisneros, Sandra. 2003. *Caramelo.* New York: Vintage Books.

Connors, Neila A. 2000. *If You Don't Feed the Teachers, They Eat the Students.* Nashville: Incentive Publications.

Daniels, Harvey. 2002. "Expository Text in Literature Circles." *Voices from the Middle* 9.6: 7–14.

Downing, Wayne. 2003. "Being Shot At Is No Fun." *Newsweek,* January 26.

Eggers, Dave, ed. 2002. *The Best American Non-Required Reading 2002.* New York: Houghton Mufflin.

Elbow, Peter. 1985. "The Shifting Relationships Between Speech and Writing." *College Composition and Communication* 35.3.

Fletcher, Ralph. 1996. *A Writer's Notebook: Unlocking the Writer Within You.* New York: Harper Trophy.

Friedman, Thomas. 2003. "Interview: Thomas Friedman Discusses Post-Saddam Middle East." *Fresh Air with Terry Gross.* Philadelphia, WHYY.

Garity, Terry. 1993. Letter to the Editor. *Austin American-Statesman*, March 27.

Geertz, Clifford. 1973. *The Interpretation of Cultures.* New York: Harper.

Gilbert, Henry. 1997. *Robin Hood.* New York: DK Publishing, Inc.

Goldberg, Natalie. 1990. *Wild Mind: Living the Writer's Life.* New York: Bantam Books.

Golding, William. 1959. *Lord of the Flies.* New York: Berkley Publishing Group.

Graves, Donald H. 2002. *Testing Is Not Teaching: What Should Count in Education.* Portsmouth, N.H.: Heinemann.

Hoban, Tana. 1990. *Exactly the Opposite.* New York: Greenwillow Books.

Homer. *The Odyssey.* 1974. New York: W. W. Norton & Company, Inc.

Hurst, James. 2000. "The Scarlet Ibis." *In The Language of Literature*, ed. Arthur Applebee et al. Evanston, Ill.: McDougal Littell.

Hyerle, David. 1996. *Visual Tools for Constructing Knowledge.* Alexandria, Va.: Association for Supervision and Curriculum Development.

Killgallon, Don. 1987. *Sentence Composing: The Complete Course.* Upper Montclair, N.J.: Boynton/Cook Publishers, Inc.

Kingsolver, Barbara. 2002. *Small Wonder.* New York: HarperCollins.

Knowles, John. 2003. *A Separate Peace.* New York: Scribner.

Koch, Kenneth. 1970. *Wishes, Lies, and Dreams: Teaching Children to Write Poetry*. New York: Random House.

———. 1990. *Rose, Where'd You Get That Red: Teaching Great Poetry to Children*. New York: Random House.

Lane, Barry. 1992. *After THE END: Teaching and Learning Creative Revision*. Portsmouth, N.H.: Heinemann.

———. 2001. *Tortoise and the Hare, Continued*. Shoreham, VT: Discover Writing Press.

———, and Gretchen Bernabei. 2001. *Why We Must Run with Scissors: Voice Lessons in Persuasive Writing*. Shoreham, VT: Discover Writing Press.

Lee, Harper. 1988. *To Kill a Mockingbird*. New York: Warner Books.

Lewis, C. S. 1985. "Letter of 26 June 1956." *C. S. Lewis: Letters to Children*. New York: Macmillan.

Luberda, James. 2004. "Anthropology and Composition: Some Notes Towards a Descriptive Composition Pedagogy." http://www.sp.uconn.edu/~jbl00001/ANTHCOMP.htm

Miller, Arthur. 1953. *The Crucible*. New York: Dramatists Play Service.

Moffett, James. 1968. *Teaching the Universe of Discourse*. Boston: Houghton Mifflin.

Montaigne, Michel de. [1580], 1958. *Essays*. J. M. Cohen, trans. Harmondsworth, England: Penguin Books.

Neider, Charles, ed. 1991. *The Complete Essays of Mark Twain*. New York: DaCapo Press.

Newkirk, Thomas. 1989. *Critical Thinking and Writing: Reclaiming the Essay*. ERIC.

———. 1997. *The Performance of Self in Student Writing*. Portsmouth, NH: Boynton/Cook.

Noden, Harry. 1999. *Image Grammar: Using Grammatical Structures to Teach Writing*. Portsmouth, NH: Heinemann.

Olsen, Tillie. 1961. "I Stand Here Ironing." *Tell Me a Riddle*. New York: Delacorte.

Olson, Gary. 1991. "Clifford Geertz on Ethnography and Social Construction." *JAC 11.2*. http://jac.gsu.edu/jac/11.2/Articles/geertz.htm

The PEN/Faulkner Foundation. 2000. *3 Minutes or Less: Life Lessons from America's Greatest Writers*. New York: Bloomsbury USA.

Rakoff, David. 2001. *Fraud*. New York: Doubleday.

Ray, Katie Wood. 2002. *What You Know by Heart*. Portsmouth, N.H.: Heinemann.

Romano, Tom. 2004. *Crafting Authentic Voice*. Portsmouth, N.H.: Heinemann.

Sewell, Anna. 1997. *Black Beauty*. New York: DK Publishing.

Shakespeare, William. 1988. *Much Ado About Nothing*. New York: Cambridge University Press.

———. 1993. *Julius Caesar*. New York: Dover Publications, Inc.

———.1993. *Macbeth*. New York: Dover Publications, Inc.

Shelley, Mary. 1984. *Frankenstein*. New York: Bantam.

Smith, Frank. 1983. *Essays into Literacy*. Portsmouth, NH: Heinemann.

———. 1998. *The Book of Learning and Forgetting*. New York: Teachers College, Columbia University.

Tovani, Cris. 2000. *I Read It, But I Don't Get It*. Portland, ME: Stenhouse.

Twain, Mark. [1876], 1986. *Tom Sawyer*. New York: Penguin.

Vowell, Sarah. 2000. *Take the Cannoli: Stories from the New World*. New York: Touchstone.

Vygotsky, Lev. 1971. "Art and Life." In *The Psychology of Art*. Cambridge, MA: MIT Press.

———. 1990. *Mind in Society: The Development of Higher Psychological Processes*. Cambridge, MA: Harvard University Press.

Warriner, John E. 1959. *English Grammar and Composition 8*. New York: Harcourt, Brace & World.

White, E. B. 1977. *Essays of E. B. White*. New York: Perennial Classics.

DISCOVER WRITING PRESS

To view our other titles
and to order more copies of

REVIVING THE ESSAY

and/or the companion CD,

LIGHTNING IN A BOTTLE

**266 visual prompts to help
students draw upon insights
for writing essays.**

visit our website at
www.discoverwriting.com

Phone: 1-800-613-8055
Fax: 1-802-897-2084

Or mail in the form below with your check, credit card or purchase order.